MondayChapel Bible
companion

MELANIE PEARLMAN

WESTBOW
PRESS®
A DIVISION OF THOMAS NELSON
& ZONDERVAN

WestBow Press books may be ordered through booksellers or by contacting:

WestBow Press
A Division of Thomas Nelson & Zondervan
1663 Liberty Drive
Bloomington, IN 47403
www.westbowpress.com
844-714-3454

Scripture quotations are taken from the Holy Bible, New International Version®, NIV®. Copyright © 1973, 1978, 1984 by Biblica, Inc.™ Used by permission of Zondervan. All rights reserved worldwide.

ISBN: 978-1-6642-9780-7 (sc)
ISBN: 978-1-6642-9781-4 (e)

Library of Congress Control Number: 2023907867

Print information available on the last page.

WestBow Press rev. date: 04/27/2023

What is "MondayChapel"?

I teach science and math to junior high and high school students. At the beginning of the second year of my employment at a Christian school in California, my principal suggested that I speak in our 8am chapel every Monday morning with a science-themed Bible lesson. Neither of us really knew what that might look like, but I agreed, enjoyed it, and continued with the assignment almost every Monday for 9 years! I came to refer to it as one word: MondayChapel. Some of the lessons turned out to be scientific explanations of events mentioned in the Bible, some were analogies using scientific principles or something in nature, and some were simply astounded praises of God's Creation! This is a compilation of many of those lessons.

What is a "Bible Companion"?

The first year I grouped MondayChapel talks into four themes: God Is Creative, God Is Big, God Has Rules, and God Created Us. But since that time, topics have widely varied across books of the Bible and scientific disciplines. So, how to arrange them, now? It turned out that I had taught on almost every book of the Bible, so I have put the lessons in that canonical order, with the intent that this book be used alongside your Bible reading. Let God's created world and His revealed Word complement each other!

Of course, you can read it front to back, if you want.

Contents

God's Artwork at the Aquarium

God blessed them and said to them, "Be fruitful and increase in number; fill the earth and subdue it. Rule over the fish in the sea and the birds in the sky and over every living creature that moves on the ground." **Genesis 1:28**

When each of my children was in 5th grade, I went on an overnight school field trip with their class to the Long Beach Aquarium, in Long Beach, CA. We learned that a horseshoe crab has copper in its blue blood (as opposed to the iron in ours, which makes ours red). It's used in medicine because of its anti-infection properties. We got to pet sharks and learned that they have an unending supply of teeth! If one falls out, it is always replaced. There were flashlight fish, who live in the depths of the ocean, with bioluminescent patches under their eyes; and comb jellies, whose gelatinous bodies bend and reflect light at the level of the wavelength of light (like the back of a CD or the surface of a soap bubble), so that they look like disco lights in the dark ocean! Such cool animals are the magnificent handiwork of our Lord! Then I noticed the words used in the aquarium signage, like "tide pool *exhibit*" and "freshwater *gallery*": those are words used in a place where works of art are displayed! Our God is a master Artist, and His works are many and wonderful to behold. And yet, in Scripture, "masterpiece" is used to describe us humans. "Masterpiece" is a word that means the best, or most well-known, or the pinnacle of an artist's career. Of all of God's Creation, we are God's *best* work. In His art gallery, we would have our own special room with spotlights on us. How do you show off God's creative skill with the way you live and use the gifts He's given you?

For we are God's handiwork, created in Christ Jesus to do good works, which God prepared in advance for us to do. **Ephesians 2:10**

When I consider Your heavens, the work of Your fingers, the moon and the stars, which You have set in place, what is mankind that You are mindful of them, human beings that you care for them? **Psalm 8:3-9**

GOD'S MUSEUM ACTIVITY

If you were going to open a museum to show off God's best creations, what would you include? Think about it for a while and then choose three things that you would feature in your museum about God. Have a friend do it, too, and then compare your answers.

Robots

Now the Lord God had planted a garden in the east, in Eden; and there he put the man he had formed. The Lord God made all kinds of trees grow out of the ground—trees that were pleasing to the eye and good for food. In the middle of the garden were the tree of life and the tree of the knowledge of good and evil… The Lord God took the man and put him in the Garden of Eden to work it and take care of it. And the Lord God commanded the man, "You are free to eat from any tree in the garden; but you must not eat from the tree of the knowledge of good and evil, for when you eat from it you will certainly die." **Genesis 2:8-9,15-17**

Did you ever wonder why God gave Adam and Eve a tree that they weren't allowed to eat from? Why not only offer good choices? Then, no sin, right? As humans, we have been given the ability to choose to do right or wrong, which is a loving offer from God. Think of it this way: If we were *unable* to do wrong, yes, we would "do right" all the time, but it wouldn't mean that we were good people - we didn't have any choice! And we wouldn't be able to love God or obey Him, we would only be choosing from a select number of right options. Robots do only what they are programmed to do. Robots cannot love, nor can they choose to obey or disobey. God wants us to love Him, and to choose to obey Him. The gift of love comes with the possibility of unloving choices, too. And sometimes we choose wrong. It's a sad part of our existence here on earth, but it means that we get to show God how much we love Him by doing what He asks of us. If there were only good choices, our obedience wouldn't mean anything.

Whoever has my commands and keeps them is the one who loves me. The one who loves me will be loved by my Father, and I too will love them and show myself to them."... Jesus replied, "Anyone who loves me will obey my teaching. My Father will love them, and we will come to them and make our home with them. Anyone who does not love me will not obey my teaching. These words you hear are not my own; they belong to the Father who sent me. **John 14:21,23-24**

This is how we know that we love the children of God: by loving God and carrying out his commands. In fact, this is love for God: to keep his commands. And his commands are not burdensome. **1John 5:2-3**

But if serving the Lord seems undesirable to you, then choose for yourselves this day whom you will serve, whether the gods your ancestors served beyond the Euphrates, or the gods of the Amorites, in whose land you are living. But as for me and my household, we will serve the Lord. **Joshua 24:15**

See also **Deuteronomy 30:11-20**

Yeast: the Fungus that Concerns a Major Jewish Holiday

That same night they are to eat the meat roasted over the fire, along with bitter herbs, and bread made without yeast... This is how you are to eat it: with your cloak tucked into your belt, your sandals on your feet and your staff in your hand. Eat it in haste; it is the Lord's Passover. **Exodus 12** (read the whole chapter! But **v. 8,11** are highlighted here)

Yeast is a one-celled organism that eats sugar and expels carbon dioxide. It is added to bread dough, where it multiplies in a warm, moist environment. Yeast provides the gas that makes bread fluffy, and wheat and eggs make stretchy layers that get filled with the gas. Yeast is responsible for the airy crumb of baked goods. But it takes some time to do its work. If you've ever baked bread, you know there is a lot of waiting involved. At the original Passover meal, when the Israelites were about to leave Egypt, God told them to make bread without yeast because they didn't have time to wait for the dough to rise; they would be leaving the country soon. Yeast comes up in the Bible, often symbolizing corruption or sin because of its growth. During the feast of Passover, even in Jewish households today, people who celebrate it abstain from eating yeast or leavening of any kind for a week, and they clean all of the leaven out of their kitchens and cupboards, remembering the haste with which the Israelites fled Egypt.

He told them still another parable: "The kingdom of heaven is like yeast that a woman took and mixed into about sixty pounds of flour until it worked all through the dough." **Matthew 13:33**

"Be careful," Jesus said to them. "Be on your guard against the yeast of the Pharisees and Sadducees."... Then they understood that he was not telling them to guard against the yeast used in bread, but against the teaching of the Pharisees and Sadducees. **Matthew 16:5-12**

YEAST ACTIVITY

Get a blank piece of paper and draw what you think yeast looks like. Then search the internet for microscope images and see how close you were.

Immune System

He said, "If you listen carefully to the Lord your God and do what is right in his eyes, if you pay attention to his commands and keep all his decrees, I will not bring on you any of the diseases I brought on the Egyptians, for I am the Lord, who heals you." **Exodus 15:26**

Do you have a scab or a bruise on your body? It's evidence of your body's God-given ability to heal itself. Our immune system senses foreign or destructive objects in our bodies and consumes them or throws them out with the waste. The sensor-driven blood-clotting mechanism keeps us from losing too much blood when we get a cut in our skin. Filters in our nose and the protective layer of skin all around us - all of these things are meant to keep sickness out of us and then attack and get rid of it when it does enter our body. God made our bodies with these amazing abilities. AND God says He, Himself will heal us when we come to Him. Sometimes that's through providing medical care. And sometimes He does it, even beyond the ways our bodies naturally work, in ways that biology and medicine can't explain. God created our bodies, surely He can change the chemistry and remove the sickness within them. Do you know how He's healed ALL of us? We have all been infected with sin (disobedience), and it's a fatal disease. Jesus' sacrifice for us on the cross has healed the sickness that would send us to hell (eternal removal from His presence). Thank you, Jesus!

As for you, you were dead in your transgressions and sins, ... But because of his great love for us, God, who is rich in mercy, made us alive with Christ even when we were dead in transgressions—it is by grace you have been saved. And God raised us up with Christ and seated us with him in the heavenly realms in Christ Jesus, in order that in the coming ages he might show the incomparable riches of his grace, expressed in his kindness to us in Christ Jesus. **Ephesians 2:1,4-7**

Praise the Lord, my soul, and forget not all his benefits— who forgives all your sins and heals all your diseases. **Psalm 103:3**

He heals the brokenhearted and binds up their wounds. **Psalm 147:3**

When John, who was in prison, heard about the deeds of the Messiah, he sent his disciples to ask him, "Are you the one who is to come, or should we expect someone else?" Jesus replied, "Go back and report to John what you hear and see: The blind receive sight, the lame walk, those who have leprosy[a] are cleansed, the deaf hear, the dead are raised, and the good news is proclaimed to the poor." **Matthew 11:2-5**

I Don't Believe in Germs

"When someone has a boil on their skin and it heals, and in the place where the boil was, a white swelling or reddish-white spot appears, they must present themselves to the priest. The priest is to examine it, and if it appears to be more than skin deep and the hair in it has turned white, the priest shall pronounce that person unclean. It is a defiling skin disease that has broken out where the boil was. But if, when the priest examines it, there is no white hair in it and it is not more than skin deep and has faded, then the priest is to isolate them for seven days. If it is spreading in the skin, the priest shall pronounce them unclean; it is a defiling disease. But if the spot is unchanged and has not spread, it is only a scar from the boil, and the priest shall pronounce them clean **Leviticus 13:18-23** (read the whole chapter - it reads like an ancient medical journal!)

Going to the dentist is not my favorite thing. But every time I go, I am thankful that I didn't live in the days when the dentist, obstetrician, orthopedist, and coroner were the same person! Physicians weren't always specialists, like we have today. They were just people who knew about the human body and how to treat diseases. The same doctor helped kids with ear infections and also moms having babies, and also broken bones, toothaches, and infectious diseases. The thing is, these doctors didn't wash their hands in between patients. I know, we cringe at this in our day, but this was all before the invention of the microscope. Think of all you know about health that these medical professionals didn't! In the 1800s, a German doctor named Ignaz Semmelweis noticed that women who gave birth with a physician attending them had a 20% mortality rate, whereas women who had midwives help (those were assistants that *only* worked with laboring moms) had a 2% mortality rate. In 1847, Semmelweis instituted hand-washing and many doctors protested; his colleagues even made fun of him. They thought it was silly to pay attention to "animals you can't see." Semmelweis was imprisoned and, ironically, died there, due to an infection. It wasn't until later in the 1800s when two scientists did some more studies, that Semmelweis' ideas had some research to back them up. Louis Pasteur introduced the idea of heating liquids to keep them from spoiling (pasteurization). And Joseph Lister suggested sterilizing instruments for surgery (you may know his name from the mouthwash brand, Listerine). What does all of this have to do with the Bible? I can think of a couple of things: 1) Just because you can't see it, doesn't mean it's not real. These "animals you can't see", or germs, caused sickness and death for thousands of years without people knowing what they were or that they were even there. 2) God took care of His people in ways they didn't know He was. The book of Leviticus was written about 3500 years ago, and in it, God gives His people rules for living including washing, quarantining the sick, and getting rid of germy items. The people he gave those commands to had no idea what salmonella, E.Coli, or black mold were! But by following God's directions anyway, they were spared sickness and death from unseen organisms at work. Thank You God for Your protection!

How many are your works, Lord! In wisdom you made them all; the earth is full of your creatures. [even microscopic ones] **Psalm 104:24**

BIBLICAL HEALTH CODE ACTIVITY

Read Leviticus chapter 13, if you haven't already. Assuming that you lived through the COVID-19 pandemic in 2020, what do you recognize from the Bible, that was also implemented during that time? If you weren't alive then, or don't remember, ask someone who does.

The Day of Atonement (Yom Kippur)

He is to lay both hands on the head of the live goat and confess over it all the wickedness and rebellion of the Israelites—all their sins—and put them on the goat's head. He shall send the goat away into the wilderness in the care of someone appointed for the task. The goat will carry on itself all their sins to a remote place; and the man shall release it in the wilderness. **Leviticus 16:21-22**

Did you know Easter is not in the Bible? I mean, Jesus' resurrection is, of course, but there are no bunnies or eggs or brunches or new dresses mentioned at all! Some holidays *are* described in the Bible. God picked out a few things He wanted His people to remember regularly, and one of those is the Day of Atonement, which happens usually in September. Every year the Jewish people would repeat the ceremony described in **Leviticus 16:21-22** and their sins were considered removed from them. The scapegoat was to be the substitute and to receive the punishment the people deserved for their sins that year. (That's what atonement means, it's making up for something, like if you ruin someone's lunch and then you replace it for them.) In English, we use the word scapegoat to mean someone you blame things on, who takes the blame for everyone else. Do you see how this holiday was a little hint about what God had in mind to accomplish through Jesus? The difference is that the scapegoat remedy was temporary and needed to be repeated every year. Jesus' sacrifice for our sins is permanent [**Hebrews 10:11-14**] Here's a worship activity you can try with your family or small group, or even by yourself. It requires a paper shredder, which will represent our scapegoat, Jesus. Take some time to think of specific sins in your life, in your family's life, in your city and country. You can write them down on some paper, or just hold a piece of paper while you think of them (when I do this with elementary students, I have them hold a piece of black paper). Many worship songs talk about how Jesus has taken the punishment for our sins. A couple I recommend are *You Are More*, by Tenth Avenue North; *You Are My King*, by Chris Tomlin; and *Reckless Love*, by Cory Asbury. Listen to these songs as you shred the papers that represent your sin and rejoice!

He is the atoning sacrifice for our sins, and not only for ours but also for the sins of the whole world. **1John 2:2**

Now God in His gracious kindness declares us not guilty. He has done this through Christ Jesus, who has freed us by taking away our sins... We are made right with God when we believe that Jesus sacrificed his life for us. **Romans 3:24-25**

Phytoplankton

The Lord spoke to Moses in the tent of meeting in the Desert of Sinai on the first day of the second month of the second year after the Israelites came out of Egypt. He said: "Take a census of the whole Israelite community by their clans and families, listing every man by name, one by one." **Numbers 1:1-2**

Do you know how to tell what the weather was like thousands of years ago? There's a way, near the ocean, to see a record of what kinds of ocean creatures lived in the long ago past. Tiny animals called phytoplankton live in the ocean (phyto means "plant" and plankton means "wanderer"). They make their own food, using sunlight, and are at the bottom of the food chain in the ocean (which means everything eats them!). They have a cell wall made of silica (which is what's in sand... and glass); this wall, sort of their skeleton, is called a frustule. Plankton rely on ocean currents and wind because they have no way to propel themselves in the water. Which type and how many plankton are in the water at any given time, depends a lot on water temperature and weather conditions. When they die, their frustules become part of what makes up the sand on the ocean floor and the beach. So, as you dig down, you see a layered account of the weather of the past. Phytoplankton skeletons give us a history of weather & climate.

Have you ever read straight through the book of Numbers? It's a toughy. There just isn't much of a story to it, or many applicable godly principles from the Lord in it. It's a book of accounting, keeping track of numbers of people and dates and families. There are other passages like this throughout the Bible, chapters or sections of chapters with genealogies (a family tree list of whose father was whose, etc.). It's tempting to skip over these sections, thinking, what good is it to read this? But like the phytoplankton, these historical records give us context for the events and people described in Scripture. Any information you know about when David lived, or who the prophets of the Old Testament were preaching to, is given from passages like this: **Luke 2:1-2; Matthew 1:2-16; Isaiah 6:1; Amos 1:1; Micah 1:1; Haggai 1:1; Zechariah 1:1; and pretty much the whole book of Numbers.**

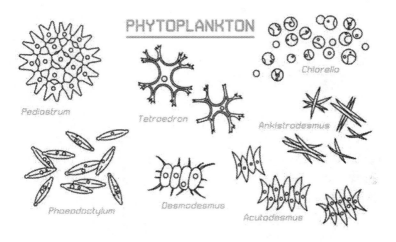

This is a royalty-free image, showing various types of phytoplankton, from istockphoto.com.

The Sound of God

Then the Lord spoke to you out of the fire. You heard the sound of words but saw no form; there was only a voice. ... You saw no form of any kind the day the Lord spoke to you at Horeb out of the fire. Therefore watch yourselves very carefully, so that you do not become corrupt and make for yourselves an idol, an image of any shape ... do not be enticed into bowing down to them and worshiping things the Lord your God has apportioned to all the nations under heaven.
Deuteronomy 4:12,15-16,19

All sound starts by vibrating molecules, which push on the molecules next to them, which push on the molecules next to them, etc., resulting in a wave of movement through air or whatever substance the sound is traveling through. Put your hand on your throat and say the sound of the letter f and then of the letter v. Then do s and z. Ch and then J. Each time, your mouth is moving the same way and the only difference is that one sound is "voiced" and one is just air passing through your throat. It's so interesting how we can *feel* sound, even though we can't see it moving. In Deuteronomy, chapter 4, God decided to reveal His nature by letting His voice be heard, instead of showing Himself. He did that so that people would not see an image and begin to worship it. Sound is not visible but it's there! God spoke the universe into being!

Now faith is confidence in what we hope for and assurance about what we do not see. This is what the ancients were commended for. By faith we understand that the universe was formed at God's command, so that what is seen was not made out of what was visible.
Hebrews 11:1-3

SOUND ACTIVITY:

Gather some cardboard tubes, better to find longer ones like those in paper towel or wrapping paper rolls, as opposed to the shorter ones for toilet paper.

Stand next to a wall, with a friend. Each of you should have one cardboard tube.

Both of you aim the tube from your body to the same point on the wall. One of you should talk into yours and the other person should hold their tube to their ear.

Experiment with aiming your tubes at different spots and see how the volume of the sound you hear changes. Be sure to switch who is talking and who is hearing.

Now aim your tubes at something softer, like a fluffy carpet, or a houseplant, or the back of the couch, and see what has changed in what you can hear.

Sound bounces off hard, flat surfaces like a billiard ball. When the surfaces are softer or bumpy, the sound doesn't reflect as efficiently or all in the same direction. The next time you're in a large auditorium, gym, or concert hall, notice the bumpy features on the walls, meant to absorb sound instead of reflect it, so that you don't hear an echo in the large room.

Ruminate Like a Ruminant

Keep this Book of the Law always on your lips; meditate on it day and night, so that you may be careful to do everything written in it. Then you will be prosperous and successful. **Joshua 1:8**

Joshua 1:5-9 says to meditate on God's Word. Nowadays, "meditate" is often used to mean emptying your mind of all thoughts, which is not what this verse means. God wants you to think about His word and consider what it means.

Cows are famous for having four stomachs. They actually have one stomach and three pre-stomachs. There is a whole class of animals for which this is true. They are called ruminants: cows, sheep, goats, buffalo, deer, elk, giraffes, and camels. The purpose of an animal's stomach is to break down the food that the animal eats and extract nutrients and water from it, for the health of the body. Cows' stomachs are huge! Go to your garage and get an outdoor "lawn and leaf"-type black garbage bag. Check to see if it holds around 30 gallons. If it does, shake it out and open it up and you'll see that its capacity is about the same as a cow's stomach! It's a slow process, digesting grass. Sometimes cows even re-chew their food to get all the nutrients out of it. Ruminants chew and chew and digest and digest until they get every little bit of good stuff out. We are to ruminate on God's word like that, chewing on it, getting everything out of it. The idea is the same: think about it, over and over. Read the context. Study the references to history or other parts of the Bible. Talk about it with other Christians. And you'll get more and more out of it.

The whole 119th chapter of Psalms is a love poem for God's Word, telling of its benefits and trustworthiness. Here's just a snippet, as a rationale for ruminating on it every day!

> I seek you with all my heart;
>> do not let me stray from your commands.
> I have hidden your word in my heart
>> that I might not sin against you.
> Praise be to you, Lord;
>> teach me your decrees.
> With my lips I recount
>> all the laws that come from your mouth.
> I rejoice in following your statutes
>> as one rejoices in great riches.
> I meditate on your precepts
>> and consider your ways.
> I delight in your decrees;
>> I will not neglect your word. **Psalm 119:10-16**

"I am with you"

Genesis 28:15; Exodus 3:12; Exodus 16; Joshua 1:5-9; Judges 6:16; Isaiah 41:10; Jeremiah 42:11; Haggai 2:4; Matthew 1:23; John 16:13

This is such a fun overview of scripture! Take the time to look up these verses in the Bible (I've listed them in the order that they show up, from beginning to end, in the way the Bible is laid out). Try to see who is speaking and who they are speaking to, in each case. What do all of these verses have in common? Isn't it comforting to see how often God has told His people that He would be with them?! These were monumental events that God promised to carry His people through. Keep in mind that in the Old Testament times, people traveled to the temple and went through a priest to communicate with the Lord. Then in the Matthew verse, we see that God sent His Son to earth, who would be known as, who personified "God with us." Then in John we see that Jesus tells about the Holy Spirit, who would come after he left, to be with us all the time! I'm so thankful to live in this time of history, when God's Spirit lives in believers all the time and I can talk to Him any time and in any place.

Answers:

Genesis 28:15 (God, to Jacob)

Exodus 3:12 (God, to Moses)

Exodus 16 (God, to Hebrews)

Joshua 1:5-9 (God, to Joshua)

Judges 6:16 (God, to Gideon)

Isaiah 41:10 (Isaiah - for God - to Israel)

Jeremiah 42:11 (Jeremiah - for God - to Israel)

Haggai 2:4 (Haggai - for God - to Zerubbabel, Joshua, and "all the people of the land")

Matthew 1:23 (an angel, to Joseph)

John 16:13 (Jesus, to his disciples)

Who is this King of Glory?

"Now appoint a king to lead us, such as all the other nations have."
1Sam. 8:5

Leader, Alpha, King, Queen, Matriarch... All of these are found in the animal kingdom: gorillas, chimps, naked mole rats, wolves, lions, bees, elephants, hyenas, and lemurs all have some sort of social order where there is selected one or more rulers over a group. Often the leader is either born into the role (as the offspring of the former leader) or animals will fight each other to find out which is strongest and then that animal will lead the rest. Silverback gorillas get groomed by others, and they eat first. Their spot is earned by strength or aggression. Chimpanzees walk first in the line, and they are bowed to by other members of their social circle. The queen naked mole rat releases hormones that keep all the other females from maturing so that the queen is the only one who reproduces. Alpha wolves mark their territory. They have the greatest freedom and they make decisions for the pack. Among lions, the largest male is the dominant one. Elephants select the oldest, and usually largest, female to be their leader. Females also lead, among hyenas. The leader is usually the largest and most aggressive and gets first access to food. Societies of people often work this way, too, where the most powerful person rules over the others. In 1Samuel chapter 8, God's people ask for a king "such as all the other nations have." And God replies, through Samuel, that a king will take their sons to serve in his army, take their daughters to serve in his household, and take portions of their crops and earnings for taxes. The people wanted this anyway, and God gave them what they wanted, but said, "they have rejected me as king." Kings in God's kingdom have not been chosen that way, nor are they necessarily the most successful or the most powerful. Jesus is our king and He reigns because He gave Himself up for us. Read the passage from Philippians chapter 2 and then sing the song, "You Are my King (Amazing Love)," by the Newsboys.

In your relationships with one another, have the same mindset as Christ Jesus: Who, being in very nature God, did not consider equality with God something to be used to his own advantage; rather, he made himself nothing by taking the very nature of a servant, being made in human likeness. And being found in appearance as a man, he humbled himself by becoming obedient to death - even death on a cross! **Philippians 2:5-8**

Who is this King of glory? The Lord strong and mighty, the Lord mighty in battle. **Psalm 24:8**

Yours, Lord, is the greatness and the power and the glory and the majesty and the splendor, for everything in heaven and earth is Yours. Yours, Lord, is the kingdom; You are exalted as head over all. **1Chronicles 29:11**

His kingdom is an eternal kingdom; His dominion endures from generation to generation. **Daniel 4:3**

> I'm forgiven because You were forsaken
> I'm accepted, You were condemned
> And I'm alive and well, Your Spirit is within me
> Because You died and rose again
> Amazing love, how can it be
> That You, my King, should die for me?
> Amazing love, I know it's true
> And it's my joy to honor You

Good Father

As for God, His way is perfect: the Lord's word is flawless; He shields all who take refuge in Him. **2Samuel 22:31**

Every living thing has a "parent" - that's part of the definition of a living thing, that it has parents from whom it inherits genes. Even carrots and amoebas, in their own way, have parents. Human beings are unique in that they need to be taken care of by their parents. We are one of the few living things whose fathers care for them. God made it this way to give us a picture of what He is like. Besides having children, what does it mean to be a *good* father? Brainstorm on paper, or with a friend, some characteristics that you think of as belonging to a good father. I hope your own father embodies at least some of these, but you can also think of other fathers you've observed or even stories of fictional fathers. God is the ultimate example of a good father (here are some of the characteristics I came up with): protecting, providing, teaching, playing, correcting, carrying, and setting an example. Read the following verses, which describe God as our Father.

"My Father, who has given [my followers] to me, is greater than all; no one can snatch them out of my Father's hand. I and the Father are one." **John 10:29**

Your Father knows what you need before you ask Him. **Matthew 6:8**

And he will be called Wonderful Counselor, Mighty God, Everlasting Father, Prince of Peace. **Isaiah 9:6**

Every good and perfect gift is from above, coming down from the Father of the heavenly lights. **James 1:17**

See what great love the Father has lavished on us, that we should be called children of God! **1John 3:1**

Dichotomous Keys and Discernment

Give Your servant a discerning heart to govern Your people and to distinguish between right and wrong. **1 Kings 3:9**

A lot of science involves putting things in categories or giving them names, so the scientific community is able to tell the difference, to discern: plants, animals, insects, clouds, tornadoes, rocks, germs, stars, galaxies, blood, fungus, soil, air, atoms, molecules all have scientific categories to them! For instance, with plants, some distinctions are easy: you can probably tell the difference between a pine tree and a palm tree. But some are a little harder. For instance, if you have these trees near you, you may be able to identify the maple, oak, or aspen trees by their leaves. But if you're not familiar with them, maybe not. There are two kinds of plants that grow in my neighborhood, and their leaves, at first glance, look almost identical! One is called an oleander - it's a large bush, often trimmed into a hedge or used to line the freeways. It's hardy, has pretty white or pink flowers, and its leaves are poisonous. Another is the California bay laurel. This is also used as a hedge, it's a large bush without flowers, but the leaves look just like oleander unless you know the difference. Bay laurels are used in cooking (ever heard of bay leaves? This plant is related to those) - you sure don't want to get these leaves mixed up! The difference is in the pattern of the veins in the leaves. Identifying plants by their characteristics and knowing the difference is important if you want to use them for a certain purpose (especially if you want to eat them!!) There are many books, called field guides or dichotomous keys, that you can use to determine what kind of plant you're looking at - it's like playing 20 questions! There are even apps that tell you what you're looking at when you take a picture. God's Word is like one of those books. Reading it helps us discern between situations that might otherwise look identical.

King Solomon asked God for wisdom and discernment, the ability to tell the difference between right and wrong. Sometimes telling the difference between right and wrong is easy: should I cheat on my taxes? Other times, I need to ask God (like it says to in James 1) and I go to the Bible (my "field guide"). God is the source of wisdom and He's written us a handbook! Just like the leaf dichotomous key helps us to discern between flavoring and poisonous leaves, the Bible helps us to discern between right and wrong.

If any of you lacks wisdom, you should ask God, who gives generously to all without finding fault, and it will be given to you. **James 1:5**

Blood Puddles

Read the account in 2Kings 3:16-18,22-23. Why did the water look like blood in the morning? Water puddles reflect the sky, and the Israelites' enemies were up early in the morning, where the rising sun colored the sky red. Our atmosphere shields us from harmful ultraviolet rays, but it also scatters the light that does come in. What's scattered most is the blue wavelengths of light (that, along with some other factors, is why the sky looks blue). At sunrise and sunset, the sun is low in the sky and the light from it is traveling through much more atmosphere, so more blue light is scattered, leaving the orange and red colors of light to reach your eye. This red light reflected off the shallow puddles of water in the ditches, and looked like the liquid in the ditches was red! God used the way His world works to help His people and carry out His plan. "Inquire of the Lord" and you may get a solution you never would have thought of on your own, but that is "easy in the eyes of the Lord."

In their hearts humans plan their course, but the Lord establishes their steps. **Proverbs 16:9**

Neverending

Give thanks to the Lord, for He is good; His love endures forever. **1Chronicles 16:34**

Look at these two geometric objects: a line and a ray, they are both eternal. That arrow on the end means that it goes on forever and ever in that direction. Forever and ever is a hard concept to understand. And talking about which of those objects is longer is even harder to understand - how can twice infinity be more than once infinity? Here's another mind-bender: 8 can be divided by 2, or by 4, to get a smaller number, but if you divide infinity by 4, it's still infinity. Infinity (the math term for "forever") is an idea, it's not a number you can count to (or that you can divide into 4 parts). We can't reach it, we can only approach it. God's Word says that He is eternal (and check out that list of Bible verses to see what else is eternal!). We may not be able to understand it, and we certainly can't reach it, but it shows how big God is, in comparison to our short lives and our small understanding. Isn't that good to know? Lots of things in this life will come to an end, but not God or our relationship with Him.

Jesus Christ is the same yesterday and today and forever. **Hebrews 13:8**

Your word, Lord, is eternal; it stands firm in the heavens. **Psalm 119:89**

He remembers His covenant forever, the promise He made, for a thousand generations. **1Chronicles 16:15**

The plans of the Lord stand firm forever, the purposes of His heart through all generations. **Psalm 33:11**

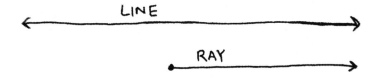

We Know the Ending - God Wins!

"Listen, King Jehoshaphat and all who live in Judah and Jerusalem! This is what the Lord says to you: 'Do not be afraid or discouraged because of this vast army. For the battle is not yours, but God's... Take up your positions; stand firm and see the deliverance the Lord will give you, Judah and Jerusalem. Do not be afraid; do not be discouraged. Go out to face them tomorrow, and the Lord will be with you.'" **2Chronicles 20:15,17**

My husband loves the Denver Broncos. He has Super Bowl 50 recorded on our TV and watches it again and again. The difference between these viewings and when he was watching it live, is that he knows the ending now. The first time, everything was unknown, but now, he focuses on the strategy of the plays and the details he missed the first 20 times he watched it, because he is assured that the game will end in victory for his team. When God first brought His people to the promised land, He told them He had given it to them (even though other people lived there at the time). Kings of Israel learned that when they worshiped God, He gave them victory against those people. In **2Chronicles 20:15**, a prophet tells King Jehoshaphat that God would give them victory against an attacking army. All of us in the world have a common, seemingly unbeatable enemy, that is death. But Jesus defeated this enemy on the cross [**1Cor 15:54-57**]! We can live forever because of him. And so we can stand firm in the face of trouble because we know the ending.

In 1981, Pope John Paul II, the leader of the Catholic Church, who lived in Italy, was shot by a criminal. He forgave his assassin, visited him in prison, and asked the people to pray for him. The Pope kept in touch with and was friends with his family. How could he do that? That's a good example that we don't need to be hateful or seek revenge, or be scared or insulted or worried because we know how the game ends! In light of my having eternal life in heaven, these other feelings just don't hold the same weight.

Take possession of the land and settle in it, for I have given you the land to possess. **Numbers 33:53**

Give us aid against the enemy, for human help is worthless. With God we will gain the victory, and He will trample down our enemies. **Psalm 60:11-12**

There is no wisdom, no insight, no plan that can succeed against the Lord. The horse is made ready for the day of battle, but victory rests with the Lord. **Proverbs 21:30-31**

When the perishable has been clothed with the imperishable, and the mortal with immortality, then the saying that is written will come true: "Death has been swallowed up in victory."

"Where, O death, is your victory? Where, O death, is your sting?"

The sting of death is sin, and the power of sin is the law. But thanks be to God! He gives us the victory through our Lord Jesus Christ. **1Corinthians 15:54-57**

Natural Selection

The earlier governors - those preceding me - placed a heavy burden on the people and took forty shekels of silver from them in addition to food and wine. Their assistants also lorded it over the people. But out of reverence for God I did not act like that. **Nehemiah 5:15**

The species, Biston betularia, also called the peppered moth, historically demonstrated a rule among organisms called "survival of the fittest:" Living things with the traits best fit for survival will live the longest, to be able to have babies with those same traits. And other living things get eaten or don't make it and so the traits they have don't get passed on. This effect is used as a basis for the theory of life evolving without the need for a Creator. Peppered moths come in a variety of speckled shades of light to dark gray, as the name implies. In the 1800s, in Europe, where the peppered moth lives, industry boomed and the amount of smoke in the air grew. Tree bark and buildings became more dingy and dark-colored. So moths that were lighter in color were more visible against these surfaces and got eaten by predators more. So the population of peppered moths gradually became darker in color, since that was the trait that survived and got passed on. Some people think, "to survive, I've got to be the strongest and only hang around with the strongest." It's a way of life or worldview, adopted by the world. God teaches us the opposite:

Be shepherds of God's flock that is under your care, watching over them... not pursuing dishonest gain, but eager to serve; not lording it over those entrusted to you, but being examples to the flock. **1Peter 5:2-3**

Jesus said to them, "The kings of the Gentiles lord it over them; … but you are not to be like that. Instead, the greatest among you should be like the youngest, and the one who rules like the one who serves. **Luke 22:25** (parallel passages in **Mark 10:42** & **Matthew 20:25**)

Flipped Upside-Down Message

Read the book of Esther, it takes about 20 minutes and is an interesting read. The account of Esther has a series of topsy-turvy events in it. An orphan who is a member of a despised minority race is chosen above others to be the queen of the land. A government official who wants to be praised ends up having to walk around town praising the man who refuses to give him the respect he thinks he deserves. That same man is hung on the very gallows he had prepared for the one he despised. Jesus' message must have sounded similar to those who first heard it: fishermen become fishers of men, Paul the persecutor becomes persecuted; those who were not a people now are a people. God works in surprising ways.

For you know the grace of our Lord Jesus Christ, that though he was rich, yet for your sakes he became poor, so that you through his poverty might become rich. **2Corinthians 8:9**

Once you were not a people, but now you are the people of God; once you had not received mercy, but now you have received mercy. **1Peter 2:10**

God made him who had no sin to be sin for us, so that in him we might become the righteousness of God. **2Corinthians 5:21**

Special Design

In His hand is the life of every creature and the breath of all mankind. **Job 12:10**

Our family's laundry basket was designed very purposefully. It has to hold as much as the washer and dryer do. Handles are helpful. Holes are good for air circulation and for reducing its weight. Special indentations on ours allow them to be stacked. There is a lower lip on one side for easier access when they are stacked. Someone, who has done laundry before, had certain features in mind and made all of these design choices for a reason. They created this basket to be the best suited for the task.

Earth's atmosphere and its place in the universe have also been designed to be well-suited for life here. The air we have is unique, compared to every other planet we've ever discovered. It's the only one that can support life. Oxygen: you might know that we need this to breathe, but did you know that too much of it would cause our bodies to overheat? And little fires start from lightning strikes all the time but go out pretty quickly. If there was more oxygen in the atmosphere, they would be fueled into bigger fires that are harder to put out. Less oxygen, of course, would make it harder to breathe. We have just the right amount. Carbon dioxide: you might know this as what we breathe out. But did you know that it also keeps our planet warm at night, like a blanket? It traps heat while the sun is on the other side of the earth. If there was less of it, all the warmth we get from the sun would radiate away during the night and it would get very cold, too cold to live. And if there was more of it, the opposite would happen, it would get too warm. Our atmosphere is just right, like it was designed with us in mind! And that's not all. There are so many other things that, if they were just a little different, life on our planet would not work. Average temperature: If it were higher, there would be more evaporation and clouds, and if it were lower, there would be more snow, which would reflect more heat and it would get colder and colder. Age of the sun: if it were older or younger, it would be less stable and the brightness would change. The rotation of the earth: If it were slower, there would be extreme temperatures during the day and night. If it were faster, there would be extreme winds, Tilt of the earth: if it were more or less, the temperature differences would be too great for us to live here. The size of the moon: the way it is keeps our axis stable. The existence of Jupiter: its gravity deflects and attracts comets that would otherwise hit our planet. Thank You, God, for designing our home for us!

God saw all that He had made, and it was very good. **Genesis 1:31**

Praise Him, all His angels; praise Him, all His heavenly hosts. Praise Him, sun and moon; praise Him, all you shining stars. Praise Him, you highest heavens and you waters above the skies. Let them praise the name of the Lord, for at His command they were created, and He established them for ever and ever. **Psalm 148:3-5**

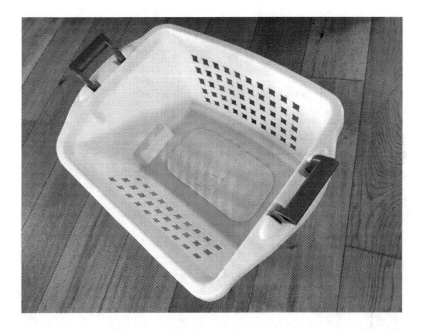

Thunderstorms

Who can understand how He spreads out the clouds, how He thunders from His pavillion? See how He scatters His lightning about Him, bathing the depths of the sea. This is the way He governs the nations and provides food in abundance. He fills His hands with lightning and commands it to strike its mark. His thunder announces the coming storm; even the cattle make known its approach. **Job 36:29-33**

Have you ever wondered why we have different kinds of weather? Why didn't God make it always sunny or always winter? Seriously, think about it for a few minutes and come up with some ideas. What about tornadoes, hurricanes, thunder and lightning? These wonders have amazed the human race for a long time, and they show us how HUGE and powerful God is. Thunder is the sound of air expanding rapidly as it is super-heated by the electric current of lightning cutting through it. During a storm there is a lot of movement of air and static electricity builds up, just like when you take off a sweater on a dry winter day. Listen to the description of the storm in the book of **Job**, one of the oldest books of the Bible. Read **36:26-29,33 - 37:7,11-14** and look for the "why." You'll see phrases like "so that" and "in order to" which give us clues about why God made thunderstorms, or at least how He uses them. I personally think that there was a storm going on as these verses were being spoken or written. Because in verse 38:1, it says "Then the Lord answered Job out of the storm." I saw the following reasons: so that we may know His work, and in order to punish men, water His earth, and show His love. I hope you're reading this at a time when you soon have the opportunity to experience a thunderstorm. Jesus had access to God's power when he was on earth and he showed it to his disciples through the calming of a storm. Their response was, "Who is this? He commands even the winds and the water and they obey him." **Luke 8:22-25**

God Is a Mystery

God's voice thunders in marvelous ways; He does great things beyond our understanding. **Job 37:5**

What's something we only know a little about? The earth's interior, the atom, black holes, the formation of the universe... we can't measure those directly, and we can only see some of them, or the effects of them. How about the ocean, for example: we know more about the craters on the moon than we do about the depths of the ocean. It's because we haven't seen much of it and it's so hard to get to. As for God, we only know what He's revealed of Himself. He reveals some of Himself through what He's created, and some by inspiring the words of the Bible for us to read. Think about it this way: I know a little about Theodore Geisel (the author that goes by Dr. Seuss) because of his writings. I know he's silly and imaginative, because of the made up words and rhymes in his books, and that he's a good artist. I know he cares about those who are weak or get picked on, because of the themes of some of his stories. But I don't know all about him, what he looks like or his wife's name. Read the Bible (God's book) and you'll find out some things about Him from that: what He cares about, and how He reacts to the ways people live. But we don't know everything about Him. He's a bit of a mystery. Make sure you read the Bible for yourself to know what God has really said, and not only what others say about Him. Also, worship God and give Him glory, whether you know how things work or not. If belief in God is based on us not knowing answers ("I don't understand it, so it must be God's doing"), then what happens when you find out the scientific explanation? That's called a "god of the gaps" and that's not who our God is!

The secret things belong to the Lord our God, but the things revealed belong to us and to our children forever, that we may follow all the words of this law. **Deuteronomy 29:29**

As big as...

Your love, Lord, reaches to the heavens, Your faithfulness to the skies. Your righteousness is like the highest mountains, Your justice like the great deep. **Psalm 36:5-6**

Mountains are big and solid. Unmoving. Really big. Look at some of the ways that mountains are thought to have formed. They all have to do with the earth's crust being "cracked" and fit together like a big jigsaw puzzle, but with the material under the puzzle being squishy and movable. The puzzle pieces are called tectonic plates, and mountains are often formed at the border of the plates, by plates lifting up, next to lowered ones, or by plates pushing together and both lifting up at the junction. Other mountains are formed by a plate being pushed in from both sides and buckling in the middle to make ripples. Some scientists say these processes took millions of years. Others see how catastrophic events on earth (earthquakes, floods, etc.) can form them much more quickly. Either way, standing on or next to mountains shows everyone that it was a huge feat! Tons of rock and dirt! Towering over the flat land! So big and high that you can't make out the details at the top! God's righteousness is compared to mountains in **Psalm 36:5-6**. What do you suppose that's saying about God's righteousness? Look at the other similes in that psalm/song. What is it saying about God's love? About God's justice?

The Abundant God of the Universe

You care for the land and water it; You enrich it abundantly. The streams of God are filled with water to provide the people with grain, for so You have ordained it. You drench its furrows and level its ridges; You soften it with showers and bless its crops. You crown the year with Your bounty, and Your carts overflow with abundance. The grasslands of the wilderness overflow; the hills are clothed with gladness. The meadows are covered with flocks and the valleys are mantled with grain; they shout for joy and sing. **Psalm 65:9-13**

There are many many verses in the Bible that speak of God's abundance of love, grace, provision, wonderful works, blessings, goodness, etc. It's a fun word study if you want to try it. Search for the words abundant, overflowing, and even "lavish" (my favorite) in the Bible. As someone who studies the Created world, I like to think about how God's creativity abounds in the universe we live in.

Do you remember coloring with an 8-color box of crayons? Probably in kindergarten. You can do fine with that. There are pretty good colors in there for almost anything you want to draw. God could have created our world like that: He could have made *a* fish, *a* flower, *a* dog, *a* fruit, *a* mountain, *a* cloud. There would still be a lot of things and we'd have a lovely place to live. But **Psalm 104:24** says "How many are Your works... in wisdom You made them all." But God went above and beyond!! It's like he used the 64-crayon box (the one with the sharpener built-in). Then there's "spring grass," "sky blue," "sea green," "forest green," and on and on, but His Creation is even better! Do you know there are 28,000 species of fish? 10,000 species of birds! Almost 300 breeds of dog! 2000 types of fruit! 10 major cloud types (though infinite shapes of them)! God's creation shows His character. He is abundantly creative, generous, abounding, overflowing! Read and think on these verses when you have some quiet moments in the coming week:

See what great love the Father has lavished on us, that we should be called children of God! **1John 3:1**

May the God of hope fill you with all joy and peace as you trust in Him, so that you may overflow with hope by the power of the Holy Spirit. **Romans 15:13**

All this is for your benefit, so that the grace that is reaching more and more people may cause thanksgiving to overflow to the glory of God. **2Corinthians 4:15**

"I have come that they may have life, and have it to the full." **John 10:10**

They celebrate Your abundant goodness and joyfully sing of Your righteousness. **Psalm 145:7**

See also **Ephesians 1:3-14**

ABUNDANCE ACTIVITY

Choose one of the following categories and list every example you can think of. Invite a friend to do it, too, and notice the similarities and differences in your lists. Here are some ideas for categories (though you could choose your own, as well): dog breeds, crayon colors, types of trees.

God's Unfailing Love

Once for all, I have sworn by My holiness - and I will not lie to David - that his line will continue forever and his throne will endure before me like the sun; it will be established forever like the moon, the faithful witness in the sky. **Psalm 89:35-37**

Because the earth we're sitting on turns around once each day, it looks to us like the sun is moving through the sky. Really, we're the ones moving and turning towards and then away from it. The amount of time it takes to turn around once is just enough for us to warm up during the day, but not get too hot, and cool off at night, but not get too cold. And because the earth we're sitting on travels around the sun once each year, tilted at a slight angle, there is a repeating pattern of seasons every year. The appearance of the sun in the sky every morning is mentioned in the Bible, many times, as an example of God's unfailing nature. [**Hosea 6:3**] Just like the sun rises and sets each day, and like we get seasons that repeat the same way every year, we know God remains the same. He is unfailing. Think about it, what other example of something so consistent and unfailing could have been written 3000 years ago, that we would still be able to relate to today? I can't think of anything. All the people and most of the civilizations from that time are long gone. Technology of that day has all been replaced, armies defeated, etc.

The words, "unfailing love" appear together many times, describing God in the Bible. Read Psalm 33, and look for that phrase, "unfailing love" in this beautiful psalm of praise!

Praise Him, sun and moon… Let them praise the name of the Lord, for at His command they were created, and He established them for ever and ever - He issued a decree that will never pass away. **Psalm 148:3, 5-6**

Satisfy us in the morning with Your unfailing love, that we may sing for joy and be glad all our days. **Psalm 90:14**

Let us acknowledge the Lord; let us press on to acknowledge Him. As surely as the sun rises, He will appear; He will come to us like the winter rains, like the spring rains that water the earth. **Hosea 6:3**

Zoom In and Out

Shout for joy to the Lord, all the earth, burst into jubilant song with music; make music to the Lord with the harp, with the harp and the sound of singing, with trumpets and the blast of the ram's horn - shout for joy before the Lord, the King. **Psalm 98:4-6**

Do you like to take pictures of nature? If you do, scroll through some of them and zoom in on detailed features. If you don't take pictures yourself, do an internet search for nature photography (I recommend nationalgeographic.com for some examples, or specifically search for Giant's Causeway in Northern Ireland, Mount Erebus in Antarctica, and The Wave in Arizona/Utah) and look at those pictures the same way. What words of description come to mind? It's likely that the words you come up with to describe these beautiful pictures are some of the same words we have in our vocabulary to describe God. You can look at pictures of neat things God made and they can speak to you without any words. That's what these Isaiah and Psalms verses are talking about. We can know a little about God by what He has made. National Geographic calls these photos "inspiring" - what do they inspire you to do? If the places you're looking at all came about by a series of unplanned explosions, collisions, and random chemical reactions, then why would they be inspiring?

The mountains and hills will burst into song before you, and all the trees of the field will clap their hands. **Isaiah 55:12**

The heavens declare the glory of God; the skies proclaim the work of His hands. Day after day they pour forth speech; night after night they reveal knowledge. They have no speech, they use no words; no sound is heard from them. Yet their voice goes out into all the earth, their words to the ends of the world. **Psalm 19:1-4**

For since the creation of the world God's invisible qualities - His eternal power and divine nature - have been clearly seen, being understood from what has been made, so that people are without excuse. **Romans 1:20**

(see also **Psalm 148:7-13**)

Bird-Watchers

Great are the works of the Lord; they are pondered by all who delight in them. **Psalm 111:2**

There is a lake near my house where I like to walk. I often see individuals or groups of people looking for birds. They are looking off into the trees. Sometimes they are smiling, taking pictures, and pointing to show each other. Almost every time I see them, I can't find what they're looking at. I feel silly trying to look in the same direction, so I often miss out. Here are the advantages that the bird-watchers have:

1. They know where to look because they know the birds' habits
2. They have tools like binoculars and bird-identification books, and they brought them with them
3. They set aside time and are patient
4. They show each other, and point out things that maybe their friend had not seen

We are God-watchers!! And I think these same four principles apply:

1. The more you know Jesus, you recognize his work, and you get to know God's "style", what He cares about **Psalm 111:1-10**
2. Our "tools" are the Bible and the Holy Spirit in us **Acts 17; John 14:26**
3. Setting aside time to be with Jesus and learn from him will give more opportunity for hearing from him. **Matthew 24:42, Psalm 130:5-6**
4. Let's point out Jesus' work to one another, to help each other see what God is doing! **Hebrews 10:24-25**

Psalm 136

Let's use a Psalm as a template to write our own praises. This psalm has a distinctive pattern to it. Read it through, first. Notice how Israel's history, the psalmist's own life, the Created world are all called in as reasons for worshiping God. This is a great praise of remembrance and a model of worship that glorifies God and is good for our soul, as well. Now, we're going to add our own experiences and feelings to this, sort of MadLibs-style. By filling in the blanks on the opposite page, you're joining in the worship service from thousands of years ago, but you can add in your experiences from today. This is just a way to get you started; feel free to keep going, beyond these lines!

Add your name in this blank:

_____ 's *Psalm of Praise*

Add different names of God that describe His character in these blanks:

Give thanks to the Lord, for He is good. His love endures forever.
Give thanks to _____ . *His love endures*
forever.
Give thanks to _____ . *His love endures*
forever.

Add attributes of God in these blanks:

To Him alone who _____, *His love*
endures forever.
who _____, *His love endures forever.*

Add things that God has done (in history or for you personally) in these blanks:

who _____ . *His love endures forever.*
He _____ *His love endures forever.*
and _____ . *His love endures forever.*
Give thanks to the God of heaven. HIs love endures forever.

Just Like Air, God Is There

Where can I go from Your Spirit? Where can I flee from Your presence? If I go up to the heavens, You are there; if I make my bed in the depths, You are there. If I rise on the wings of the dawn, if I settle on the far side of the sea, even there Your hand will guide me, Your right hand will hold me fast. **Psalm 139:7-10**

I bet you never thought about how a straw works and that it requires the whole atmosphere to get that liquid goodness in you! You suck some air out from the inside of the straw and then the atmospheric pressure, which is now greater than the pressure inside the straw, pushes the liquid up through the straw and into your mouth. We don't usually think about air being all around us all the time, being pressed down on by the miles of atmosphere above us. But it is. All the time. Between your foot and your sock, inside your body, and between the hairs on your head. Likewise, you may not think much about God being everywhere, either. The Bible says God is with us all the time, Isn't it good to trust a God who isn't constrained by space and time? If that were true, waiting your turn to talk to Him would take forever! What reminders can you put in place so that you think about that more?

For I am convinced that neither death nor life, nor angels nor demons, neither the present nor the future, nor any powers, neither height nor depth, nor anything else in all creation, will be able to separate us from the love of God that is in Christ Jesus our Lord. **Romans 8:38-39**

Read **Acts 10**, looking for how God was in many places at once.

STRENGTH OF THE ATMOSPHERE ACTIVITY

Here is a magic trick you can do, that uses the strength of atmospheric pressure. Get a drinking cup and a poker card that is bigger than the opening of the cup. Fill the cup all the way to the top with water and put the card on top, making sure that it completely covers the cup's mouth. Carefully (and maybe over a sink, especially the first time you do it) hold the card firmly to the mouth of the cup and turn everything upside down. You should be able to let go of the card and see that the water and card stay just where they are. Because there is no air inside the cup, only water, the atmospheric pressure pushing up on the card is greater than the weight of that small amount of water. Pretty cool, right?

Biomimicry

Praise the Lord. Praise the Lord from the heavens; praise Him in the heights above. Praise Him, all His angels; praise Him, all His heavenly hosts. Praise Him, sun and moon; praise Him, all you shining stars. Praise Him, you highest heavens and you waters above the skies. Let them praise the name of the Lord, for at His command they were created. **Psalm 148:1-5**

What do Velcro, a carpenter's level, and a Japanese bullet train have in common? Part of the design of each was inspired by nature. The engineering of God's Creation is remarkable and God's handiwork is shown over and over again. Engineers throughout human history, and still today, research how the details of nature can be reproduced or used in other tools for our benefit. A quick internet search for each of these below will show you how man-made objects and tools look and behave and why the design from God's Creation was copied.

- How a penguin removes salt from sea water -> desalination plant
- The hydrodynamics of a Kingfisher (bird) beak -> Japanese high-speed train
- Lightweight flight of "Helicopter" maple seeds -> remote controlled Nano Air Vehicle
- Movement and position-sensing semicircular canals in our ears -> carpenter's level
- Efficient water transport in Calla lily petals -> water mixing paddle
- Phosphorescent animals and plants -> glow in the dark stickers

- Iridescent butterfly wings -> LED screens
- Burrs that carry seeds -> velcro
- Extra sticky gecko feet -> shoes for walking on wet rocks
- Mussels attaching themselves to rocks under water -> waterproof glue

The amazing properties of the Created world shouldn't compel us to worship those things, but rather the Creator of them. Glory to God!

Bones

A heart at peace gives life to the body, but envy rots the bones. **Proverbs 14:30**

Look at this diagram of the inside of the human bone: it's very strong and slightly flexible, because of what it's made of and relatively lightweight, because of the less dense material inside. Your body is constantly re-growing, replacing cells, recycling parts, and taking out dead cells from your bones. That's why they can heal when they're broken. Really, all doctors do is make sure a broken bone is aligned like it's supposed to be and isn't able to move, and your body is what does the mending. Healthy bones are central to our well-being. They hold us up and protect our important parts. Unhealthy bones make for a miserable existence. The Old Testament books of Psalms and Proverbs use bones to describe how you're doing deep inside (sort of like our sayings, "from the bottom of my heart" or "a feeling in my gut.") Take some time to read these passages: **Psalms 32:3, 42:10, 109:18, 139:13-14; Proverbs 3:8, 12:4, 15:30, 16:24.** Notice that many of these maladies are things we can control in our actions: envy, hiding sin, teasing or cursing. Are you thinking about the effect on other people's bones when you speak or act?

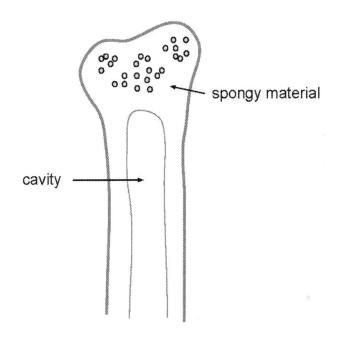

spongy material

cavity

The Heavens

I applied my mind to study and to explore by wisdom all that is done under the heavens… I tried cheering myself with wine, and embracing folly - my mind still guiding me with wisdom. I wanted to see what was good for people to do under the heavens during the few days of their lives… There is a time for everything, and a season for every activity under the heavens. **Ecclesiastes 1:13, 2:3, 3:1**

Why does the Bible so often refer to things in the sky as "the heavens"? In the time in history when the Bible was written, people thought the earth was flat, the sea was the edge of the earth and not crossable, the Sun went around the earth, and the sky was in layers, one layer contained the moon, another had assorted planets, another the sun, and another the stars. So when Paul mentions the "third heaven," [**2Corinthians 12:2**] he's probably referring to the third level of concentric spheres that were part of his understanding of the world. Anytime Biblical authors mention "the heavens," they mean all of those layers. It's like when we say we see Jupiter in the sky, even though it's not in our atmosphere as clouds are "in the sky" - it's millions of miles away - but appears to be a dot of light right next to that cloud.

Lord, our Lord, how majestic is Your name in all the earth! You have set Your glory in the heavens. **Psalm 8:1**

He made the earth by His power; He founded the world by His wisdom and stretched out the heavens by His understanding. **Jeremiah 51:15**

I know a man in Christ who fourteen years ago was caught up to the third heaven. **2Corinthians 12:2**

He who descended is the very one who ascended higher than all the heavens, in order to fill the whole universe. **Ephesians 4:10**

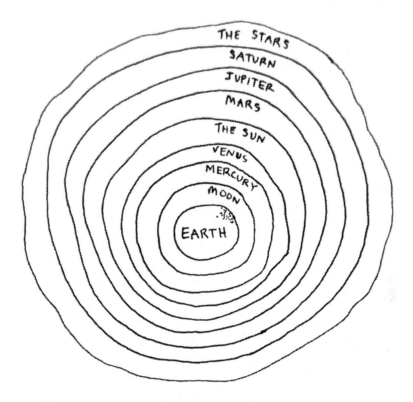

This drawing shows Earth and its atmosphere at the center and, as you go out: the moon, Mercury, Venus, the Sun, Mars, Jupiter, Saturn, and then the stars. Each was thought to reside in its own sphere which encircled the Earth. (Interestingly, these seven layers of the heavens are where we get the days of the week: Moon = Monday, Sun = Sunday, Saturn = Saturday, and Tuesday through Friday are derived from the Norse names of the planets Mercury through Jupiter.)

Scientific Root Words

Do you not know? Have you not heard? The Lord is the everlasting God, the Creator of the ends of the earth. He will not grow tired or weary, and His understanding no one can fathom. **Isaiah 40:28**

The study of science includes a lot of big words. The good news is that most of them are made up of smaller parts that, when you know what they mean, help you to understand the meaning of the bigger word. For example, "photosynthesis" is made of "photo," which means light, and "synthesis" which means put together. It's the process by which a plant puts together its food using light from the sun. When the word fragment "able" is found at the end of a word, it means able to do whatever is in front of it. I read a food package that had the word "nonovenable" printed on it. Now, I don't think that's a real word, and I had never seen it before. But, I could tell, because I knew that "non" means not and "able" means able to, that it meant the package was not able to be put in the oven.

A favorite song of mine has a lot of big words in it: "Indescribable," by Chris Tomlin. Picking apart that big-word title, we see God is not able to be described. Can you think of anything else you know of that is not able to be described? The other words in the song say that He is not able to be held in a container, or compared to anything we can see. Enjoy these verses from the book of Job, which say the same thing:

Where were you when I laid the earth's foundation? Tell me, if you understand. Who marked off its dimensions? Surely you know! Who stretched a measuring line across it? On what were its footings set, or who laid its cornerstone - while the morning stars sang together and all the angels shouted for joy?

Who shut up the sea behind doors when it burst forth from the womb, when I made the clouds its garment and wrapped it in thick darkness, when I fixed limits for it and set its doors and bars in place, when I said, "This far you may come and no farther; here is where your proud waves

Have you ever given orders to the morning, or shown the dawn its place, that it might take the earth by the edges and shake the wicked out of it?...

Have you journeyed to the springs of the sea or walked in the recesses of the deep? Have the gates of death been shown to you? Have you seen the gates of the deepest darkness? Have you comprehended the vast expanses of the earth? Tell me, if you know all this.

What is the way to the abode of light? And where does darkness reside? Can you take them to their places? Do you knw the paths to their dwellings? Surely you know, for you were already born! You have lived so many years!

Have you entered the storehouses of the snow or seen the storehouses of the hail, which I reserve for times of trouble, for days of war and battle? What is the way to the place where the lightning is dispersed, or the place where the east winds are scattered over the earth?

Who cuts a channel for the torrents of rain, and a path for the thunderstorm, to water a land where no one lives, an uninhabited desert, to satisfy a desolate wasteland and make it sprout with grass?...

Can you bind the chains of the Pleiades? Can you loosen Orion's belt? Can you bring forth the constellations in their seasons or lead out the Bear with its cubs? Do you know the laws of the heavens? Can you set up God's dominion over the earth?

Can you raise your voice to the clouds and cover yourself with a flood of water? Do you send the lightning bolts on their way? Do they report to you, "Here we are"? Who gives the ibis wisdom or gives the rooster understanding? Who has the wisdom to count the clouds? Who can tip over the water jars of the heavens when the dust becomes hard and the clods of earth stick together? **Job 38:3-38**

Where Do Rivers Come From?

My people have committed two sins: they have forsaken me, the spring of living water, and have dug their own cisterns, broken cisterns that cannot hold water. **Jeremiah 2:13**

Do you know that all rivers around the whole world flow in the same direction? Yup, downhill. Have you ever thought about where rivers begin?. A spring or wellspring is the start of a river, often coming right out of a hillside. [See the percolation discussion regarding Jeremiah 17] Man can't create a wellspring - it's a factor of having enough rain to start an underground flow of water, and then the right geology under the ground, to guide that water to a place where it can "spring" out. A cistern, however, is manmade. It is a large container that holds water (you might call it a tank). Cisterns are important in the life of an ancient Israeli village because they hold water in between the infrequent rains. They really are a life-saver, to have water stored in the middle of the dry desert. In Jeremiah chapter 2, the prophet describes other "cisterns" that are broken, that the people were trying to depend on (we try to store up joy with friends, parties, good weather, job offers, but it doesn't last). A cistern only holds so much water, and a broken cistern, even less. But going to the source of a river, that's a lot of water! Jesus never runs out of supply! God describes Himself as the spring of living water. He is a wellspring of the joy of living! Read these two verses of the hymn, Joyful Joyful, We Adore Thee, written by Henry Van Dyke:

Joyful, Joyful, We Adore Thee, God of glory, Lord of love
Hearts unfold like flowers before Thee, opening to the Sun above
Melt the clouds of sin and sadness; Drive the dark of doubt away;
Giver of immortal gladness, Fill us with the light of day!

Always giving and forgiving, Ever blessing, ever blest,
Wellspring of the joy of living, Ocean-depth of happy rest!
Loving Father, Christ our Brother, Let Your light upon us shine;
Teach us how to love each other, Lift us to the joy divine.

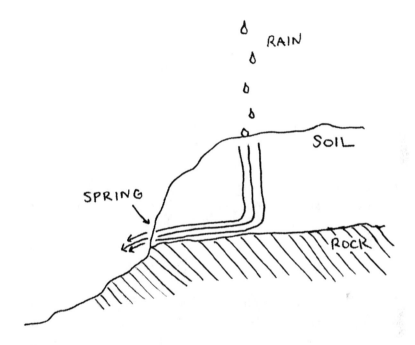

Planted by Streams of Water

But blessed is the one who trusts in the Lord, whose confidence is in Him. They will be like a tree planted by the water that sends out its roots by the stream. It does not fear when heat comes; its leaves are always green. It has no worries in a year of drought and never fails to bear fruit. **Jeremiah 17:7-8**

Take a look at this diagram of what happens when it rains. Water "percolates" down into the soil until it reaches a place where it can't go any farther. At that point, the water builds up, just like filling a bathtub. As more rain falls, the underground water level rises. It's called the "water table." In spots where the surface of the land has depressions or fissures, it's possible to see the ground level lower than the water table level. This is how we get lakes, streams, and rivers. So you can see why a tree planted near a stream grows well - that means it's very close to a water supply. Would a tree by a stream be in danger if it was really hot outside and it was losing water through its leaves? Would it be in danger if it didn't rain for a few months? No! Even during times of drought or heat, the tree has established access to water.

This is like trusting in the Lord. Spending time with Jesus and reading the Bible is like planting yourself right by that supply of hope and peace and love and joy. When times are difficult, you've already established that connection with the Wellspring of Life. Notice that the Bible *doesn't* say that when you trust in the Lord there will always be rain, or that the temperature will stay a nice 75 degrees. But in the face of whatever conditions, the supply of life-giving water is right there!

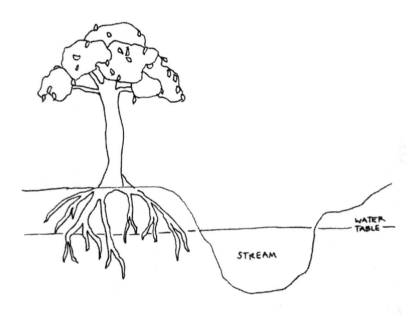

STREAM

WATER
TABLE

Solar System Scale

Ah, Sovereign Lord, you have made the heavens and the earth by Your great power and outstretched arm. Nothing is too hard for You. **Jeremiah 32:17**

My eighth-grade science class designs a scale model of the solar system every year, to install somewhere on our school's campus. The sizes of planets and the distances between them are HUGE numbers, hard to even comprehend. When we shrink them down, we get a better idea about how big some planets are, compared to others, and also about which planets are closer together and which are more spread out. We also learn about God, the Creator of our Universe, that He must be huge! Every year we learn that a model of planet sizes and planet distances could not use the same scale (for instance, 1 inch = 10,000 miles), because either the smallest planet would be too small to see, or the farthest planet(s) would not fit on our school's campus!

For since the creation of the world God's invisible qualities - His eternal power and divine nature - have been clearly seen, being understood from what has been made, so that people are without excuse. **Romans 1:20**

Entropy

Yet this I call to mind, and therefore I have hope: Because of the Lord's great love we are not consumed, for His compassions never fail. They are new every morning; great is Your faithfulness. I say to myself, "The Lord is my portion; therefore I will wait for Him." The Lord is good to those whose hope is in Him, to the one who seeks Him; it is good to wait quietly for the salvation of the Lord. **Lamentations 3:21-26**

Can you think of something that you've had for a long time? Do you remember what it looked like when it was new, compared to now, maybe today it's kind of shabby and worn-out? You can usually tell by looking at an item whether it has been through more time on earth, in this system of increasing disorder. The 2nd law of Thermodynamics states that disorder always increases in a closed system. A scattering of pennies won't, on their own, arrange themselves into neat stacks. A cup of coffee sitting on the counter won't heat itself back up. That's what the second law of thermodynamics means. We decay and so does everything else that's made. In Lamentations 3, the prophet Jeremiah is "lamenting" (complaining) about the brokenness of the world and the difficulty of his job as a prophet. Look at the imagery he uses, and the sad phrases in verses 21-26. But be encouraged by this passage in 2Corinthians. There is hope for us who know Jesus!

Therefore we do not lose heart. Though outwardly we are wasting away, yet inwardly we are being renewed day by day. For our light and momentary troubles are achieving for us an eternal glory that far outweighs them all. So we fix our eyes not on what is seen, but on what is unseen, since what is seen is temporary, but what is unseen is eternal. **2Corinthians 4:16-18**

Praise be to the God and Father of our Lord Jesus Christ! In His great mercy He has given us new birth into a living hope through the resurrection of Jesus Christ from the dead, and into an inheritance that can never perish, spoil or fade. **1Peter 1:3-4**

ENTROPY ACTIVITY

If you want to see entropy for yourself, find a thermometer that can measure between body temperature and boiling water. Make a hot cup of tea or cocoa, or just heat up some water and take its temperature right away and write it down. Decide on an interval of time in which you're willing to keep measuring. Every 3 minutes, let's say. Measure the temperature again after 3 minutes and write it down. Keep this up until the temperature no longer changes. It might be interesting to try it again and start with different initial temperatures, to see what's different. Or try it on a day that's much cooler or warmer.

One Percent

For this is what the Sovereign Lord says, "I myself will search for my sheep and look after them. As a shepherd looks after his scattered flock when he is with them, so will I look after my sheep. I will rescue them from all the places where they were scattered on a day of clouds and darkness." **Ezekiel 34:11-12**

If you have 100 of something, usually it's not valuable enough that one of them would be missed very much if you lost it: 100 pennies, 100 M&Ms, 100 paper clips, or even 100 dollars! One out of a hundred isn't much, 1%. Jesus tells about a shepherd who cares so much for his 100 sheep, that he goes after one who is missing, when he still has 99 who are safe. I guess it's more like a 100-piece puzzle. If you're missing a piece of that, the puzzle can't be completed. The piece is unique and important enough that the puzzle isn't finished without it. Jesus' story says that there is much rejoicing when the lost one is found. It's good to have a God, like that shepherd, who pursues us and cares for us. We can live that way, as well, caring for others enough to go after them when they are in trouble and help even just one.

Suppose one of you has a hundred sheep and loses one of them. Doesn't he leave the ninety-nine in the open country and go after the lost sheep until he finds it? And when he finds it, he joyfully puts it on his shoulders and goes home. Then he calls his friends and neighbors together and says, "Rejoice with me; I have found my lost sheep." **Luke 15:4-6**

God Is Trustworthy

If we are thrown into the blazing furnace, the God we serve is able to deliver us from it, and He will deliver us from Your Majesty's hand. But even if He does not, we want you to know, Your Majesty, that we will not serve your gods or worship the image of gold you have set up. **Daniel 3:17-18**

Do you know someone who constantly tells lies or who doesn't follow through on what she said she would do? It's hard to trust someone like that. There is the famous fable from Aesop (who lived just before Jesus' time. Jesus might have known his fables!) about the boy who cried "wolf!" The people of his village eventually don't believe anything he says, because he has a history of lying to them. It works the same in reverse: if you are someone who is known to tell the truth, then people will generally believe you and trust you. In an even sillier example, I have a friend that is such a good cook, I'll eat anything she makes, even if it's a food I don't normally like, because she has proven to me that her cooking makes anything taste good!

God keeps His promises, that's one of His character qualities. How do we know that? Read the accounts of His interactions with His people. Talk to God-followers that you know. Yes, there are times when God doesn't do the things I want. But that doesn't mean He isn't trustworthy - He never promised me that dream job or that perfect relationship. We can learn a lot about God's trustworthiness and also about trusting Him, from the book of Daniel. When Daniel and his friends faced trouble, they turned to God. Daniel's response was to pray. He didn't know if God would rescue him, or do what he asked, but He knew God was able and that God does what's best. There is great perspective in focusing on what God has promised us, knowing that He will remain true to those promises forever. I will trust in You whether I get what I want or not!

The Lord gave and the Lord has taken away; may the name of the Lord be praised. **Job 1:21**

The Lord gives victory to His anointed. He answers him from His heavenly sanctuary with the victorious power of His right hand. Some trust in chariots and some in horses, but we trust in the name of the Lord our God. **Psalm 20:6-7**

Twice Fulfilled

As he came near the place where I was standing, I was terrified and fell prostrate. "Son of man," he said to me, "understand that the vision concerns the time of the end." **Daniel 8:17**

Reading the book of Daniel is interesting and difficult. Visions and prophecies in Daniel have been fulfilled in our history, for instance, a prophecy in chapter 8 was fulfilled 400 years later, through a later king of Persia. Daniel's vision described his behavior, how he'd come to power, and the bad things he would do. But parts of the vision also have yet to be fulfilled when Jesus returns. In a timeline-of-history sense, fulfillment looks one way, but in a spiritual-eternity sense, it looks another way. It reminds me of looking at things through a microscope. Magnify it and the same item looks different. (For fun, search online for images of dust, shark skin, kosher salt, and a compact disc, all under a microscope!)

For thousands of years, people could only see with their own eyes. Then microscopes were invented and a whole other world was opened up. What intricate Creation God has made, that we can rediscover the world we know at a microscopic level! There is another passage, that might sound more familiar to you, which has a double fulfillment: Psalm 22. King David had a rough life. We don't know when he wrote this, but he was feeling awful, and he still knew that God was in control. Jesus quoted Psalm 22:1 from the cross. Listen to the other parts of the Psalm: verses 7, 16-18 give a good description of his situation, and they were written 1000 years beforehand! For a thousand years, God's people knew this Psalm as David's pain and hope in the Lord. And then Jesus spoke it, and coming from his mouth, we hear it a different way. Let's thank God for how He orchestrated all this. His plan was in place before David was even born.

For everything that was written in the past was written to teach us, so that through the endurance taught in the Scriptures and the encouragement they provide we might have hope. **Romans 15:4**

Posterity will serve him; future generations will be told about the Lord. They will proclaim his righteousness, declaring to a people yet unborn: He has done it! **Psalm 22:30-31**

Stork Migration

Return, Israel, to the Lord your God. Your sins have been your downfall! Take words with you and return to the Lord. Say to Him: "Forgive all our sins and receive us graciously, that we may offer the fruit of our lips." **Hosea 14:1-2**

What is the longest road trip you have ever been on? Do you know which way is north, from where you are right now? There are many animals who travel far every year, and who know their north from south, even though they don't have Google Maps! The Bible mentions the stork, which is a migratory bird that would fly over Israel every year on its trip from Europe to Africa and back. The European stork is about 3.5 feet tall and has a 5-foot wingspan. It squeezes water out of moss to give to its chicks. It poops on its own legs to cool them off when it's hot. Storks spend their summers in Europe and have their babies there, and then they spend the winter in Africa. They fly very high and very far, sometimes 8000 miles (over twice the width of the continental United States). We don't know how animals know which way to fly. Maybe God gave them a sense of the earth's magnetic field, or they watch the sun's path? The prophet Jeremiah also had this message for God's people, to take a lesson from the stork. It was a call to repentance, which means to reverse direction and head back to God. Repentance is something that happens when you first decide to follow Jesus (John the Baptist's message was for the Jews to repent of their sins). And it's also something we continue to do whenever we've gone away from the Lord. Birds do it by instinct. We have to make the choice. And we don't wait for summer. God wants us to return to Him every time we make a wrong decision, whether it's a little mess-up or 8000 miles off course.

"When people fall down, do they not get up? When someone turns away, do they not return? Why then have these people turned away? Why does Jerusalem always turn away? They cling to deceit; they refuse to return. I have listened attentively, but they do not say what is right. None of them repent of their wickedness, saying, 'What have I done?' Each pursues their own course like a horse charging into battle. Even the stork in the sky knows her appointed seasons, and the dove, the swift and the thrush observe the time of their migration. But my people do not know the requirements of the Lord." **Jeremiah 8:4-7**

In those days John the Baptist came, preaching in the wilderness of Judea and saying, "Repent, for the kingdom of heaven has come near." **Matthew 3:2**

God Is Light

Do not gloat over me, my enemy! Though I have fallen, I will rise. Though I sit in darkness, the Lord will be my light. Because I have sinned against Him, I will bear the Lord's wrath, until He pleads my case and upholds my cause. He will bring me out into the light; I will see His righteousness. **Micah 7:8-9**

Light is a wave of electrical and magnetic energy that can travel through a complete vacuum. It travels in a straight line until it encounters a boundary of the medium it's traveling in. Darkness is the absence of light. You can't turn on dark. You can't open a box of darkness and make light disappear. But you can turn on light and then darkness is not dark anymore. Light waves can either be reflected (as I just described, it's like a ball bouncing off a wall), absorbed (in which case, there is no light reflected and we don't see it), or it can pass through objects (as in the case of a window or some clear water). It allows us to see things, only by bouncing off of those things and then entering our eyes, to produce an image on the back of our eyeball, which is then interpreted by our brain. In the Bible, light stands for understanding, and uprightness. And the absence of light (darkness) represents confusion or evil intentions. Enjoy these passages that make three points about light:

1. GOD IS LIGHT - **1John 1:5; 2Samuel 22:29; Psalm 119:105,130;**

2. JESUS BROUGHT LIGHT TO EARTH - **John 1:5; John 8:12; Ephesians 4:18;**

3. WHEN WE HAVE JESUS IN OUR HEARTS, WE ARE LIGHTS, TOO! - **Psalm 4:6; 1John 1:6; Ephesians 5:8**

JOY

Though the fig tree does not bud and there are no grapes on the vines, though the olive crop fails and the fields produce no food, though there are no sheep in the pen and no cattle in the stalls, yet I will rejoice in the Lord, I will be joyful in God my Savior. **Habakkuk 3:17-18**

In John chapter 15, we have the account of when Jesus used the analogy of a grapevine, saying that we are branches and that the fruit we produce is only because we are connected to the vine. Botanically, he's spot on! If you cut a branch off the vine, it will no longer produce any fruit - the branch gets all of its water and nutrients from the vine and its connection to the soil and the photosynthesizing leaves. What's neat is what Jesus then says about why he made this point. It's in verse 11: "I've told you about abiding so that your joy may be complete." We can have complete joy when we stay in a relationship with Jesus because he provides and nourishes and enables us to grow and bear fruit! Happiness is an emotion that changes with our circumstances. But joy is a state of being that doesn't change and can be "complete," even when our day-to-day experience is sad or difficult or discouraging. This is a fun visual, that J.O.Y. is when there's 0 between Jesus and You. Find the most joy-filled worship song you know and sing about it! Keep reading for more Bible verses about our joy in the Lord!

Remain in me, as I also remain in you. No branch can bear fruit by itself; it must remain in the vine. Neither can you bear fruit unless you remain in me. I am the vine; you are the branches. If you remain in me and I in you, you will bear much fruit; apart from me you can do nothing... I have told you this so that my joy may be in you and that your joy may be complete. **John 15:4-5,11**

Rejoice in the Lord always. I will say it again: Rejoice! **Philippians 4:4**

I am coming to you [God the Father] now, but I say these things while I am still in the world, so that they may have the full measure of my joy within them. **John 17:13**

Blessed are those whose transgressions are forgiven, whose sins are covered. Blessed is the one whose sin the Lord will never count against them. **Romans 4:7-8**

I keep my eyes always on the Lord. With Him at my right hand, I will not be shaken. Therefore my heart is glad and my tongue rejoices; my body will also rest secure, because You will not abandon me to the realm of the dead, nor will You let Your faithful one see decay. **Psalm 16:8-10**

The Wonder of Water

On that day, living water will flow out from Jerusalem, half of it east to the Dead Sea and half of it west to the Mediterranean Sea, in summer and in winter. The Lord will be king over the whole earth. On that day there will be one Lord, and His name the only name. **Zechariah 14:8**

Water is essential for all life. Water molecules, like everything else, have electric charges in them. A unique thing about water, though, is that the positive charges tend to bunch up on one side of the molecule and the negative charges tend to bunch up on the opposite side. That's why water dissolves things, gets things clean, and helps digest food in your body. Those electric charges help to break up some other substances. All life forms on our planet need water - that's why when scientists look for life on other planets, they always start by looking for evidence of water. Humans can only survive a couple of days without taking in any water (you could go a few weeks without food). God and Jesus both called themselves the source of living water. It's a good metaphor because we need water so much and we can't live without it! The woman at the Samaritan well that Jesus met was doing her job for her family. Imagine living in a desert where it didn't rain between May and November, and there was no plumbing. Getting water was a daily requirement that meant survival. Jesus tells her that he has living water to give her. The woman's encounter with Jesus changed her and her whole town! Telling people about Jesus is like saying, "I found water!" to someone dying of thirst.

Lord, You are the hope of Israel; all who forsake You will be put to shame. Those who turn away from You will be written in the dust because they have forsaken the Lord, the spring of living water. **Jeremiah 17:13**

As the deer pants for streams of water, so my soul pants for You, my God. My soul thirsts for God, for the living God. Where can I go and meet with God? **Psalm 42:1-2**

"If you knew the gift of God and who it is that asks you for a drink, you would have asked him and he would have given you living water... Everyone who drinks this water will be thirsty again, but whoever drinks the water I give them will never thirst. Indeed, the water I give them will become in them a spring of water welling up to eternal life. **John 4:10,13-14**

ELECTRIC WATER ACTIVITY

In order to see the electrical nature of water, blow up a latex balloon and take it to a sink. Rub the balloon on your hair, so that you build up a static electric charge on the balloon. Then turn on the sink, but just barely, so that there's a thin steady stream of water coming out of it. Hold the charged side of the balloon near the stream of water and you should see the water bend toward or away from the balloon. The electrical charge on the balloon is reacting to the electrical charges in the water!

Hiding in Plain Sight

You are the light of the world. A town built on a hill cannot be hidden. Neither do people light a lamp and put it under a bowl. Instead they put it on its stand, and it gives light to everyone in the house. In the same way, let your light shine before others, that they may see your good deeds and glorify your Father in heaven. **Matthew 5:14-16**

Camouflage is used by animals to blend in and not be noticed, either for defensive or offensive purposes. Chameleons and cuttlefish are well-known examples. Do you ever try to hide by blending in? It might look like:

- Being quiet when we should speak up
- Going along with the crowd, when you know they're wrong
- Denying that you follow Jesus because it's not popular
- Letting sin make our lives look the same as that of unbelievers
- Not giving God the glory He deserves, in front of other people
- Ignoring the needs of others because caring for them would be "drastic"

As Christians we are NOT to hide or blend in. We *will* stand out from our surroundings. Jesus said not to cover our light but to set it on its stand, so everyone can see it. Here are a couple of examples from the Bible, the first negative and the second positive:

When Zimri saw that the city was taken, he went into the citadel of the royal palace and set the palace on fire around him. So he died, because of the sins he had committed, doing evil in the eyes of the Lord and following the ways of Jeroboam and committing the same sin Jeroboam had caused Israel to commit. **1Kings 16:18-19**

Then they called them in again and commanded them not to speak or teach at all in the name of Jesus, but Peter and John replied, "Which is right in God's eyes: to listen to you, or to Him? You be the judges! As for us, we cannot help speaking about what we have seen and heard." **Acts 4:18-20**

First Things First

But seek first His kingdom and His righteousness, and all these things will be given to you as well. **Matthew 6:33**

Jesus taught, in his sermon on the mount, not to worry about possessions, money, clothes, or the future, but to "seek first His kingdom," as quoted above. Here is my visual representation of Jesus' teaching (see the photo of the jars.) This is a common time management demonstration. The goal is to put all of the rice and all of the balls into the jar. However, if you put the rice in first, the balls won't fit. If you put the balls in first, the rice settles around the larger balls, and fits into the spaces between the balls. The point of this visual is that when we make little, unimportant things a priority, sometimes that doesn't leave room for the main things. It's better to make time for the important things first, and then those little extras will have enough room, as well. Jesus warns us not to let less important things fill our minds and hearts and time, but to seek him first. Our relationship with him is the most important thing. Jesus' parable of the four soils also tells of the seed that fell among thorns and how the thorns were like the worries - and even pleasures - of this life can choke out the health of our faith in the Lord. In Psalm 37, David says that as we seek the Lord and delight in Him, our desires become His desires, the desires for His Kingdom (the things He rules over and cares about). During certain unstructured times of life, I often set up these jars in my house as a reminder to put first things first.

The seed that fell among thorns stands for those who hear, but as they go on their way they are choked by life's worries, riches and pleasures, and they do not mature. **Luke 8:14**

Take delight in the Lord, and He will give you the desires of your heart. **Psalm 37:4**

Let the peace of Christ rule in your hearts, since as members of one body you were called to peace. And be thankful. Let the message of Christ dwell among you richly as you teach and admonish one another with all wisdom through psalms, hymns, and songs from the Spirit, singing to God with gratitude in your hearts. And whatever you do, whether in word or deed, do it all in the name of the Lord Jesus, giving thanks to God the Father through him. **Colossians 3:15-17**

Teach us to number our days, that we may gain a heart of wisdom. **Psalm 90:12**

The Ribbon of Gold

"The kingdom of heaven is like a mustard seed, which a man took and planted in his field. Though it is the smallest of all seeds, yet when it grows, it is the largest of garden plants and becomes a tree, so that the birds come and perch in its branches." **Matthew 13:31-32**

Yes, a mustard seed is small, about 1mm in diameter (that's about the thickness of your fingernail). It's not technically the smallest of all seeds, but it is the smallest of agricultural seeds used in the ancient near east. The plant is large, in comparison with the seed - it can grow to six feet high. And it is a hardy plant; it grows quickly, without being cultivated by man. It's a weed, in the town where I live. Wild mustard is native to the Mediterranean basin but is found in climates that are similar to that, all over the world. Because it's so hardy, and because it can outcompete native plants, it is considered an invasive species where it spreads or is planted. There is a legend that Father Junipero Serra, a Spanish monk who established missions all along the coast of what is now the state of California, planted mustard seeds as he walked from mission to mission. He did that so that when he made the return trip the following spring, there would be a "ribbon of gold," a path of that prolific yellow flowering plant, that could guide him, and anyone who wanted to travel from mission to mission. That's some quick growth! Think of how the Christian Church has grown in just 2000 years, from a small group of Jesus' followers to millions!

But you will receive power when the Holy Spirit comes on you; and you will be my witnesses in Jerusalem, and in all Judea and Samaria, and to the ends of the earth. **Acts 1:8**

Losing To Save

What good will it be for someone to gain the whole world, yet forfeit their soul? Or what can anyone give in exchange for their soul? **Matthew 16:26**

If you had to choose one of these for a whole week, which would you choose?

Have a pet mouse or a pet baby crocodile?
Only wear pajamas or only go barefoot?
Have to take a nap everyday or have to eat broccoli every day?
Only have access to Netflix or only have access to YouTube?

How would your answers change if the commitment was for a year? In the verses around Matthew 16:26, Jesus was telling Peter that he was making decisions, based only on this life. If you make choices, only thinking about your time on earth, they center around your comfort and happiness, maybe your possessions - and lots of people live this way. Peter was saying no, Jesus, you need to live a long time and fix things here, keep healing and turning people to God. But Jesus could see eternal life and what he could do for people of all time by dying on the cross. If *you* made choices based on eternal life, what would look different? What's important isn't what's comfortable now, but what pleases the Lord, and what lasts forever.

Have you ever caught a lizard and had it detach its tail and run away? Daddy Longlegs spiders and some other animals can do that, too. God gave them special muscles around certain joints that can pinch off parts of their body without losing a lot of blood. It's harder to live without that limb, but they get to stay alive. The reasoning for the animals is that it's better to lose this tail or this leg than to die now. Jesus says it's better to give up the comforts of the world now (money, popularity, the best toys) and make sure your soul is with God forever. Read also through Matthew 6:25-34 and see if you can hear what are the things of this world and what are the things that last forever.

Recycling

When the Son of Man comes in his glory, and all the angels with him, he will sit on his glorious throne. All the nations will be gathered before him, and he will separate the people one from another as a shepherd separates the sheep from the goats. **Matthew 25:31-32**

Sorting what goes into the trash versus the recycle bin happens completely depending on what the item is made of, not how useful or successful it was. A waxed cardboard milk container, no matter how useful it might still look, or how good of a job it did keeping my milk fresh, still cannot be recycled (at least by my city's recycling program) because of the materials used to make it. On the other hand, a plastic yogurt container, which held yucky yogurt I didn't like and whose lid kept coming off when it wasn't supposed to, will be recycled because it is made of the right kind of plastic. Jesus talks about separating sheep and goats, and wheat and weeds, both used as metaphors for judgment at the end of our lives. In the same way as recycling, people will be sorted according to whether they knew Jesus, not on how well they lived or how good they were.

If anyone acknowledges that Jesus is the Son of God, God lives in them and they in God. **1John 4:15**

Whoever has the Son has life, whoever does not have the Son of God does not have life. **1John 5:12**

Therefore, if anyone is in Christ, the new creation has come: The old has gone, the new is here! **2Corinthians 5:17**

In Christ you are a new creation, made fit for the Kingdom. If you haven't told the Lord you want to live for Him, and you do, you can pray any time. I'm going to write a sample of words you can use, and you can pray them along with me - or use your own words. *Dear God, thank You for sending Your Son to die in my place so that I can come to You. I'm sorry for the times I go my own way. I want to accept Your gift and live for You.* If you've prayed this type of prayer for the first time today, please tell another Christian about it!

Storm on the Sea of Galilee

A furious squall came up, and the waves broke over the boat, so that it was nearly swamped... He got up, rebuked the wind and said to the waves, "Quiet! Be still!" Then the wind died down and it was completely calm... They were terrified and asked each other, "Who is this? Even the wind and the waves obey him!" **Mark 4:37,39, 41**

The Sea of Galilee, found in northern Israel, is a place where Jesus spent a lot of time during his ministry on earth. Many of his disciples were from towns around this lake and had grown up on its shores. At some point in his time with them, Jesus sent his disciples across the lake in a boat without him, when a sudden storm kicked up. This is common on the Sea of Galilee. It's 680 feet below sea level, and surrounded by hills, except for a gap on the western side, where wind enters and then whips around inside this geologic bowl. I recommend looking at GoogleEarth, at the Sea of Galilee, and dropping into a "street view" right in the middle of the lake. Then, look around you. Jesus walks out to the boat, on top of the water, and then speaks to the wind and waves to quiet them. He used this to show his disciples that he was God, in control of the weather. Read the Psalm 107 passage - it's the same scene! Jesus is showing that he is the same God praised in the Psalms. What does this mean for us? We can trust God. The scene is in Psalm 107 and our response is found in Psalm 104:

Some went out on the sea in ships; they were merchants on the mighty waters. They saw the works of the Lord, His wonderful deeds in the deep. For He spoke and stirred up a tempest that lifted high the waves. They mounted up to the heavens and went down to the depths; in their peril their courage melted away. They reeled and staggered like drunkards; they were at their wits' end. Then they cried out to the Lord in their trouble, and He brought them out of their distress. He stilled the storm to a whisper; the waves of the sea were hushed. They were glad when it grew calm, and He guided them to their desired haven. Let them give thanks to the Lord for His unfailing love and His wonderful deeds for mankind. **Psalm 107:23-31**

I will sing to the Lord all my life; I will sing praise to my God as long as I live. May my meditation be pleasing to Him, as I rejoice in the Lord. **Psalm 104:33-34**

Jesus Was Born in April?

Today in the town of David a Savior has been born to you; He is the Messiah, the Lord. **Luke 2:11**

The reason we celebrate the birth of Christ at the end of December has an interesting history. You may know that the earth's path around the sun causes the tilt of the earth to point towards the sun for half the year and then away from the sun for the other half. As the tilt is headed away from the sun, the days get shorter and shorter. The shortest amount of sunlight in one day (in the northern hemisphere, anyway) falls on December 21 or 22. This is called the winter solstice. Right after that, the tilt starts heading back towards the sun and the hours of daylight per day begin to get longer. Even before watches, calendars, or telescopes, people noticed this phenomenon. Those who worshiped the sun as a god attributed this to the sun being reborn at the end of December. December 25 was a pagan celebration of the birth of the sun. Christians who lived during this time didn't want to worship the sun and they decided instead to celebrate the birth of the Son (of God, Jesus). Historically, Jesus was likely born in a time when it was fair weather for traveling in Israel (because Caesar asked everyone to travel to their family's hometown), and also when shepherds would be watching their sheep in the fields at night, which usually occurred during the time when sheep are having their lambs (late spring). For these reasons, it's likely that Jesus was born in April. That's ok, right? Haven't you had a birthday party that wasn't on your actual birthday?

The Word became flesh and made his dwelling among us. We have seen his glory, the glory of the one and only Son, who came from the Father, full of grace and truth. **John 1:14**

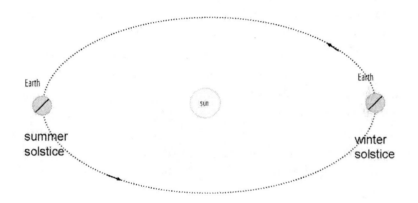

Earth

summer
solstice

sun

Earth

winter
solstice

Weather Prediction From the First Century

"When you see a cloud rising in the west, immediately you say, 'It's going to rain,' and it does. And when the south wind blows, you say, 'It's going to be hot,' and it is. Hypocrites! You know how to interpret the appearance of the earth and the sky. How is it that you don't know how to interpret this present time?" **Luke 12:54-56**

Jesus quotes this popular weather prediction pattern among the fishermen and farmers of ancient Galilee. For an area of the world where the weather moves from west to east, it makes sense that clouds in the western sky would be the best predictor of foul weather headed your way. And where would a south wind be coming from? Saudi Arabia and Egypt! It's a pretty good bet that those places would supply dry, hot wind. While we can't know the weather exactly, even with our advanced technology today, we can see some signs of what's coming. And even without satellite imagery and barometric readings, the people of Jesus' day had some idea of what to expect of the weather in the near future. Jesus used this to describe his coming, that there would be signs, some idea of what to expect, though we wouldn't have a certain or exact prediction.

"When evening comes, you say, 'It will be fair weather, for the sky is red,' and in the morning, 'Today it will be stormy, for the sky is red and overcast.' You know how to interpret the appearance of the sky, but you cannot interpret the signs of the times." **Matthew 16:1-3**

Triple Point

"Anyone who loves me will obey my teaching. My Father will love them, and we will come to them and make our home with them... All this I have spoken while still with you. But the Advocate, the Holy Spirit, whom the Father will send in my name, will teach you all things and will remind you of everything I have said to you."
John 14:23,25-26

One of my favorite science demonstrations is to play with dry ice. Dry ice is carbon dioxide that is so cold, what is normally gas at room temperature turns to solid. This happens at -109 degrees Fahrenheit. You can find dry ice at some grocery stores, it's used to add to a cooler to keep food extra cold (like if you wanted to transport frozen food). Dry ice is also used to make "fog" effects. At room temperature, or especially when you add warm water to it, dry ice goes straight from a solid to a gaseous state. This is called sublimation. Normally, a substance goes from solid to liquid to gas, as temperature increases. And under certain conditions, a substance will only exist in one of those states. There is, however, a special circumstance, where solid, liquid and gas all occur under the same conditions. This is called a triple point. For water, this point is at 0.01 degrees Celsius (pretty close to the normal freezing point of water) and 0.006 atm pressure (about 200 times less than atmospheric pressure at sea level). Though it seems impossible to our everyday experience, the three states can exist at the same time. Some scientists say this is like the trinity of God: He is Father, Son, and Holy Spirit, and one God. That's a hard concept to understand. Jesus described it for his disciples in the John 14 passage. A chemist may describe it like this: one substance, water, can be found in three states: solid, liquid and gas.

Fruit

Remain in me, as I also remain in you. No branch can bear fruit by itself; it must remain in the vine. Neither can you bear fruit unless you remain in me. **John 15:4**

Most of us call fruit any plant you'd eat as a snack or that is sweet. And we call a vegetable any plant you'd put in a salad. But the real definition of a fruit is biological. It's the part of the plant that holds the seeds; it is how a plant makes more of itself. Fruits are usually sweet because animals are more likely to eat the fruit and then spread the seeds around, if the fruit is sweet and juicy. If you are like a plant, then the things you say and do and make are your fruit. We can't produce fruit on our own - we need to stay connected to Jesus!

You will eat the fruit of your labor **Psalm 128:2**

They will eat the fruit of their ways and be filled with the fruit of their schemes. **Proverbs 1:31**

By their fruit you will recognize them. Do people pick grapes from thornbushes, or figs from thistles? Likewise, every good tree bears good fruit, but a bad tree bears bad fruit. A good tree cannot bear bad fruit, and a bad tree cannot bear good fruit. **Matthew 7:16-18**

Necessity of the Gardener

"I am the true vine, and my Father is the gardener. He cuts off every branch in me that bears no fruit, while every branch that does bear fruit he prunes so that it will be even more fruitful."
John 15:1-2

Picture weeds in your yard. What do they look like? In my yard, palm trees, tomato plants, California poppies, grass, and roses have all been weeds. Weeds are not a type of plant, but rather a plant that's not part of the plan, no matter how beautiful or useful it is thought to be. The gardener has a plan, knows what s/he wants, where. My favorite flower is the California poppy. I love seeing it bloom each year, especially in mass quantities. However, I have a path in my yard, and I don't want poppies springing up in the middle of the path. So even though it's a native species and it's my favorite flower, I will pick it from the middle of the path, so that the path is cleared off. When there's not a gardener, plants grow over each other, outside their boundaries, and choke each other out or get too big for their own health. They can spring up in places that are not good growing environments. Planting and pruning, according to the plan of the gardener, makes for the healthiest and most beautiful gardens. This passage says that Jesus is the vine and God is the gardener. God has a finished garden design in mind and He prunes and weeds, in order to match that design. It's hard for me to pull poppies, because I like them so much. They're not bad plants, but if they're messing up the greater picture of the yard, they have to go. I got an opportunity to go to a science convention, which is a good thing - I really enjoy those and always learn a lot! But as I thought and prayed about it, I really got a sense that it wasn't for the good of my family, and I didn't go. Not all good things are the best things. Are there things in your life that aren't necessarily bad, but they are not part of God's plan? Trust the Gardener's plan and pull out those things that don't belong, or are crowding the plants that are supposed to be featured; pull them out while they're little and easy to get!

WEEDING THE GARDEN ACTIVITY

Take some time to think and pray through your habits, pastimes, and commitments. Are any of them in the overgrown poppies category: beautiful, but in the wrong place, or crowding out the plan for the garden? If you're not sure, talk with someone who knows you well. And, of course, go to the Gardener!

God Is an Artist

The God who made the world and everything in it is the Lord of heaven and earth and does not live in temples built by human hands. And He is not served by human hands, as if He needed anything. Rather, He Himself gives everyone life and breath and everything else. From one man He made all the nations, that they should inhabit the whole earth; and He marked out their appointed times in history and boundaries of their lands. God did this so that they would seek Him and perhaps reach out for Him and find Him, though He is not far from any one of us. **Acts 17:24-27**

God is an Artist who plans, makes design choices, and skillfully puts it all together. He chooses a medium, colors, style, details, and how to present his art. In that sense, I call God an artist when I look at certain things He's made. The camel, for instance, is so well-suited for its environment! Camels have long eyelashes and hairy ears - this keeps sand from going into those holes in their heads. They have a hump of fat that weighs around 80 lbs, where energy is stored for long stretches without food. Everywhere else on their body, they are lean, to keep their overall weight down. Camels' feet are large, and well-suited for walking on sand. They can open and close their nostrils, also to keep sand out. And they don't sweat, so they are able to conserve the water in their body in very hot and dry conditions. Camels can change their body temperature between 93 and 107 degrees Fahrenheit, and cool the blood that goes to their brain. They have thick lips and can eat prickly desert plants without injuring their mouths and throats. A camel's forehead sticks out like a visor, to shade its eyes from the sun. This animal was masterfully designed and arranged for the place where it lives. How else do we see God making choices for His creation that fit them perfectly for their environment? Not all art is pretty, but it's all made for a purpose. You are God's handiwork, too, His masterpiece, created to do good things!

For we are God's handiwork, created in Christ Jesus to do good works, which God prepared in advance for us to do. **Ephesians 2:10**

Combinations In the Crowd

The God who made the world and everything in it is the Lord of heaven and earth and does not live in temples built by human hands. And He is not served by human hands, as if He needed anything. Rather, He Himself gives everyone life and breath and everything else. From one man He made all the nations, that they should inhabit the whole earth; and He marked out their appointed times in history and boundaries of their lands. God did this so that they would seek Him and perhaps reach out for Him and find Him, though He is not far from any one of us. **Acts 17:24-27**

In my prealgebra class, we learn how to find the number of combinations of toppings on a pizza or outfits in a closet by multiplying. There's a great resource on khanacademy.com that shows how the movie production company, Pixar, makes crowds of robots or monsters, using this same process. They mathematically combine a number of possible body parts. Need a bunch of different-looking robots? Ten kinds of heads, 10 kinds of bodies, and 10 kinds of legs yields 1000 unique robots! (See algebra *is* useful after 8th grade!) Some people believe that our lives, our personalities, and our circumstances are completely determined by chance like this. Do you feel like a random combination of traits, mixed up in the genes inherited from your parents? The Bible says that is not the case. Read these verses that tell about God's purposeful design and His involvement in our lives and circumstances.

For You created my inmost being; You knit me together in my mother's womb. I praise You because I am fearfully and wonderfully made; Your works are wonderful, I know that full well. My frame was not hidden from You when I was made in the secret place, when I was woven together in the depths of the earth. Your eyes saw my unformed body; all the days ordained for me were written in Your book before one of the them came to be. **Psalm 139:13-16**

"Before I formed you in the womb I knew you, before you were born I set you apart; I appointed you as a prophet to the nations." **Jeremiah 1:4-5**

In Him we were also chosen, having been predestined according to the plan of Him who works out everything in conformity with the purpose of His will. **Ephesians 1:11**

Indeed, the very hairs of your head are all numbered. Don't be afraid; you are worth more than many sparrows. **Luke 12:7**

My Kids' Artwork

For since the creation of the world God's invisible qualities - His eternal power and divine nature - have been clearly seen, being understood from what has been made, so that people are without excuse. **Romans 1:20**

I have kept this kindergarten art, made by my son, who is now in college, for many years, now. Why? Is it because it's so lifelike? Because of the beautiful composition? No, it's because it reminds me of him when he was five. It reminds me of what he was like at that age. He liked making things according to a plan or picture, and he liked realistic things (this is a model of the outer, middle, and inner ear, can't you tell?) The things he made tell about what he was like, what he was interested in, and how he liked to work. That's why I love to learn about science. I like to study things that God has made because they tell about what He is like: massive, creative, orderly, and purposeful. The sun rising and setting, waves in the ocean and seasons repeating every year are all evidence of God's consistency, God could have shown us that He is unchanging by making His creation unchanging. But He chose to display His creativity at the same time. So autumn arrives at the same time every year, but we get to experience variety in the course of a year, also.

The heavens declare the glory of God; the skies proclaim the work of His hands. Day after day they pour forth speech; night after night they reveal knowledge. They have no speech, they use no words; no sound is heard from them. Yet their voice goes out into all the earth, their words to the ends of the world. **Psalm 19:1-4**

The heavens praise Your wonders, Lord, Your faithfulness too, in the assembly of the holy ones. For who in the skies above can compare with the Lord? Who is like the Lord among the heavenly beings? **Ps 89:5-6**

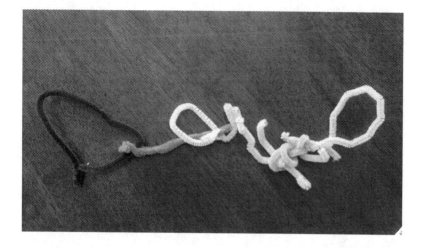

Force Diagrams

I do not understand what I do. For what I want to do I do not do, but what I hate to do. And if I do what I do not want to do, I agree that the law is good... For I have the desire to do what is good, but I cannot carry it out. For I do not do the good I want to do, but the evil I do not want to do - this I keep doing... For in my inner being I delight in God's law; but I see another law at work in me, waging war against the law of my mind and making me a prisoner of the law of sin at work within me. **Romans 7:15,18-19, 22-23**

See the diagrams with arrows, showing how when multiple forces act on an object, the greatest one wins and determines its acceleration. Gravity overcomes buoyancy and a pulling force overcomes friction. The apostle Paul writes in his letter to the Romans, that he feels that way, pulled in two directions by the Spirit and his sinful nature. "I want to be good, I know that's the best course. But I like having things my way, doing them for myself." That's a struggle and it can be frustrating. I'm sure you can relate to this - I can! I have good intentions to be generous, but then I like to do things for myself. I want to be kind and inviting, but then that person makes me uncomfortable and it's easier to stick with my friends. Sometimes I make good choices and sometimes they are bad. So what, then, if my good outweighs my bad, then I'm ok? Is that how it works, whichever force pulls harder wins? If the net force points towards heaven then I'm saved? Here is Paul's answer:

What a wretched man I am! Who will rescue me from this body that is subject to death? Thanks be to God, who delivers me through Jesus Christ our Lord! v.24-25!

Thanks be to God! We've been rescued from this tug of war. By believing in Jesus we are innocent in God's eyes. The good choices now are out of thankfulness for His salvation, not us trying to measure up.

For the flesh desires what is contrary to the Spirit, and the Spirit what is contrary to the flesh. They are in conflict with each other, so that you are not to do whatever you want... But the fruit of the Spirit is love, joy, peace, forbearance, kindness, goodness, faithfulness, gentleness and self-control. **Galatians 5:17,22-24**

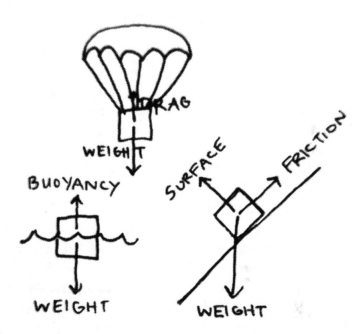

Skeletal Joints in the Human Body

There are different kinds of gifts, but the same Spirit distributes them. There are different kinds of service, but the same Lord. There are different kinds of working, but in all of them and in everyone it is the same God at work. **1Corinthians 12:4-6**

Look at these four different types of joints that are found in your body: your knee, your spine, your shoulder, and your wrist. There are benefits and drawbacks to each type. The hinge joint in the knee is very strong and sturdy. But it isn't very flexible, it can only bend one way, and through a limited angle. The pivot joints in the spine are extremely flexible and allow the trunk of your body to bend and move in many ways. It's also protective of the nerves in the spinal cord. Your shoulder has a very wide range of motion. And your wrist also can move in many directions, but is more delicate and can't bear much weight.

What if your knees didn't bend, and you wanted to play basketball? What if your fingers couldn't wiggle and you wanted to peel an orange? What if your back had to be straight all the time, and you needed to tie your shoes? The body of Christ is like this. Its parts work differently, and we are created for different reasons and purposes, and each of us has special features. And together we make up the church. Are you thankful for the unique way God created you? Have you found how your characteristics and talents fit into the larger picture of the church? May we bring glory to God in how we work together!

For just as each of us has one body with many members, and these members do not all have the same function, so in Christ we, though many, form one body, and each member belongs to all the others. **Romans 12:4-5**

ALL KNEES ACTIVITY

What if all of the joints in our bodies were like our knee joints: only bending in one direction, with range of motion from straight to a little past 90 degrees? Take some time to think, write, or draw about what would be different about our daily activities and abilities.

Möbius Strip

Love never fails. But where there are prophecies, they will cease; where there are tongues, they will be stilled; where there is knowledge, it will pass away. **1Corinthians 13:8**

This fun math demonstration shows an eternal surface. Follow the directions to make a möbius strip, and then draw a line along the middle of the surface. If you keep drawing and don't pick up your pen, you'll see that you arrive back at the same place. This shape only has one surface, yet it's made of paper that has two surfaces! Here are some directions to make a neat surprise with these.

Make another möbius strip, but twist the paper in the opposite direction as you did on the first

Attach the two together at right angles
Cut them down the middle of the strip

You'll get two hearts, entwined. Awwww… God's love is eternal. The Bible mentions that often: **Psalm 108:4; Romans 8:35-39; John 17:21-26; Lamentations 3:22; Ephesians 3:18-19** Listen to the song lyrics of *One Thing Remains*, by Brian Johnson, Jeremy Riddle and Christa Black Gifford. It's based on 1Corinthians 13, but has ideas from some of these other passages, as well. Prophecy, tongues, and knowledge will pass away, they will end, but God's love never fails, never ends.

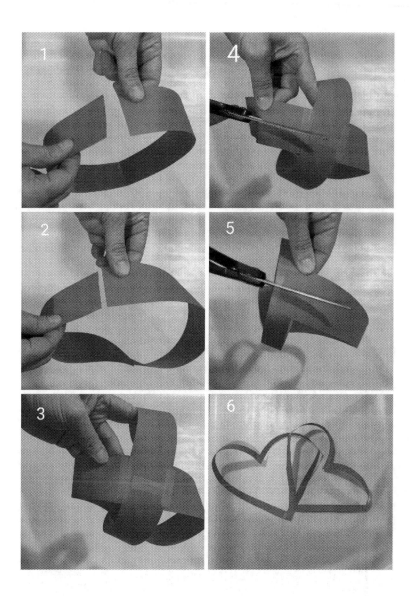

Smell

For we are to God the pleasing aroma of Christ among those who are being saved and those who are perishing. To the one we are an aroma that brings death; to the other, an aroma that brings life. **2Corinthians 2:15-16**

This is a fun game to play: put some items in opaque containers (I use brown paper bags or jars that aren't see-through) and have someone try to guess what they are by smelling them, only. Items I recommend are: soap, popcorn, bacon, banana, pencil shavings, onion, cinnamon, coffee, mustard, gum or candy, grass, and baby powder. What an interesting sense, our smell! When you smell something, molecules that can evaporate from that thing actually enter your nose. There are chemical sensors at the base of your brain that can recall the shape of the molecule the last time you smelled that thing, and they send the message to your brain, which interprets that it's baby powder or broccoli or coffee. We can distinguish 10,000 different odors, so it's a hard subject to study. We do know, though, that smell is very closely linked to memory. Paul tells us to be like a smell to others, an aroma of Jesus. What does that mean? Using this metaphor, we are little pieces of Jesus, we bring Jesus' love, forgiveness, and truth so that we "smell" like him. It means that when people encounter us, it should remind them of what they know of Jesus. To people who don't know him, it may be stinky, but to those who are ready to hear about Jesus, it's a beautiful fragrance.

Remember this image when
You visit family
You go to work or school
You talk to the waiter at the restaurant
You spend time at the airport
You attend church
You are asked to help out

Are you being an aroma of Christ?

A New Creation!

Therefore, if anyone is in Christ, the new creation has come: The old has gone, the new is here! **2Corinthians 5:17**

I think you can't fully appreciate springtime unless you live in a place where it snows all winter. The landscape is cold and dead for months. Nothing grows, not very much is green, and there is less wildlife to see outside as animals hibernate or just stay in shelters more of the time. Spring shows us new flowers and growth, baby animals, and the outside world seems to have come alive again with new birth. Eggs, grass, and bunnies are often a symbol of spring, the time when Easter happens. When Jesus rose from the dead, it really was in the springtime of the year, but the bunnies and eggs and grass are just symbols of that time of new birth. Why do we use symbols of new birth? Because Jesus made us a new creation by dying for our sin!

But because of His great love for us, God, who is rich in mercy, made us alive with Christ even when we were dead in transgressions - it is by grace you have been saved. **Ephesians 2:4-5**

Poor Detectors

We do not dare to classify or compare ourselves with some who commend themselves. When they measure themselves by themselves and compare themselves with themselves, they are not wise... For it is not the one who commends himself who is approved, but the one whom the Lord commends. **2Corinthians 10:12,18**

This is a fun experiment: one student puts a hand in warm water and one in cold, for a few minutes. Then they each put that same hand in a bowl of room-temperature water. It will feel cold to the first one and warm to the other. Your body is so good at adjusting and adapting to its surroundings, which is good, but it makes us a lousy judge of things. Have you ever walked out of a dark movie theater and the sunlight was blinding? Your body had adapted to the dark and needs a few minutes to readjust to daylight. If you want an accurate reading of temperature, use a thermometer. The same is true with our feelings: if we are sad, we tend to be more sensitive to other people's words. If we are angry, maybe we're more likely to be mean. If we're hungry, we can be impatient with other things that don't have anything to do with food. The Bible tells us that our heart is easily swayed and biased, and so can make us poor judges of right and wrong. God's Word is a good thermometer. Comparing things against it can tell us if they are right or wrong, rather than just going with how you feel.

The heart is deceitful above all things and beyond cure. Who can understand it? **Jeremiah 17:9**

"You are the ones who justify yourselves in the eyes of others, but God knows your hearts. What people value is highly detestable in God's sight." **Luke 16:15**

A person may think their own ways are right, but the Lord weighs the heart. **Proverbs 21:2**

Resonance

Since we live by the Spirit, let us keep in step with the Spirit.
Galatians 5:25

Do you know this trick? Fill a wine glass partially with water, wet
your index finger slightly, and then run it around the rim of the
glass, holding onto the bottom with the other hand. It will take
some experimenting with the amount of pressure you apply and the
speed with which you move your finger, but you should hear the
glass "singing" a note. The reason this happens is that your finger
is vibrating the glass at its resonant frequency. All objects have a
certain frequency (or frequencies) at which they shake more, than
at others. Bang a chair on the ground, drop a pot on the floor, and
you'll hear a "GONG" or "CLANG" that's always the same note.
If you can reinforce that same frequency, the sound will re-sound,
louder and clearer. As Christians, we want to resonate with the Holy
Spirit. A list of what the Spirit produces is given just a few verses
before the one we're looking at today. "The fruit of the Spirit is love,
joy, peace, patience, kindness, goodness, faithfulness, gentleness
and self-control." That's what we want to tune ourselves to, to keep
time with. Walking with Jesus means that we move in sync with his
movement. We walk like he did, we love like he does, our "sounds"
should re-sound his "sounds."

Chicken Egg

Praise be to the God and Father of our Lord Jesus Christ, who has blessed us in the heavenly realms with every spiritual blessing in Christ. **Ephesians 1:3** (read also **verses 4-14**)

How closely do you look at your breakfast? A chicken egg has a protective shell that allows for gases to pass through it. Inside, the egg white (called the albumen) is a squishy thick liquid that protects the growing chicken from slamming against the shell, and it also contains protein for the chicken's growing body. There is a membrane around it and it's just small enough for some air to fit between it and the shell, providing the baby chicken's first breath. The egg yolk has more protein and fat, which are food for the baby chicken as it grows and develops. If you look more closely, you see a white dot on the yolk, called the germ. This is where the baby chicken develops, it contains the information (the recipe, if you will) for the chicken's development. There is also a squiggly white thread-looking structure, called the chalaza, which tethers the baby chicken to the yolk, keeping it in the middle, away from the hard shell, as its fragile body develops. Crack an egg into a bowl and look for all of these parts! Also, once the baby chicken is ready to hatch, it uses a special hook that grows on its tiny beak. It's called an egg tooth and is useful for making the initial break in the shell so the baby chicken can escape its growing chamber. The egg provides everything the baby chicken will need, just as God provides all we need to live for Him. Read this passage in Ephesians and list all of the things you see in there that God has provided for us! The Holy Spirit helps us live for God. The good news, the message, God's plan revealed to us; this is the way God communicated to us. He gives us understanding and wisdom, and the starting place of forgiveness and grace. He gives us a purpose: to belong to Christ, to be holy and without blame, to be God's child, and to bring praise to His glory! The chicken egg (and Ephesians 1) show that God plans ahead and provides for His creation. We have all we need to live for Him!

Command those who are rich in this present world not to be arrogant nor to put their hope in wealth, which is so uncertain, but to put their hope in God, who richly provides us with everything for our enjoyment. **1Timothy 6:17**

His divine power has given us everything we need for a godly life through our knowledge of Him who called us by His own glory and goodness. **2Peter 1:3**

Symbiosis: Commensalism and Parasitism

For it is by grace you have been saved, through faith - and this is not from yourselves, it is the gift of God - not by works, so that no one can boast. **Ephesians 2:8-9**

There are two types of symbiosis (this word means "together living") among organisms on earth. One is called commensalism, which is a mutually beneficial relationship between two organisms. An example of this would be the zebra, the wildebeest, and the ostrich, who all feed together on the African savanna. The zebra has good hearing, which the other two animals don't. The wildebeest is the best smeller. And the ostrich has height and great eyesight. Between the three of them, they are more likely to be alerted to approaching danger, than any would, on its own. Another type of symbiosis is parasitism, which is when there is a relationship between organisms, but only one of them benefits from it and the other is actually harmed. This is like a tick living on your skin, or a tapeworm in your intestines, getting nutrients from your body instead of allowing the nutrients to benefit your body. Also, the plant mistletoe is a parasite. Its seeds get spread around by birds, and when they land on a tree branch, they imbed and sprout and start to get the nutrients from the tree, instead of out of the ground, like other plants. Which of these symbiotic relationships is like our relationship with Jesus? Ephesians 2:8-9 says that we are only saved through what Jesus did for us and that there is nothing we can do to earn the right to be in relationship with God. We are more like the tick than the zebra, getting all of the benefit, at his expense. The difference is that Jesus welcomes our parasitic relationship, and even designed us for it. When we say "in Jesus' name" at the end of a prayer, it's acknowledgment that we know we can only come before God because of Jesus.

10 Little Rubber Ducks, by Eric Carle, and the real event that happened on January 10, 1992

Then we will no longer be infants, tossed back and forth by the waves, and blown here and there by every wind of teaching and by the cunning and craftiness of people in their deceitful scheming. **Ephesians 4:14**

A cargo ship, carrying crates of toys from Hong Kong to Tacoma, Washington, encountered a storm in the Pacific Ocean. Some of the wares on that ship ended up in the ocean, including 29,000 bath toys, and for months and years, rubber ducks turned up on beaches all around the world. The duckies floated with the currents as shown in the map. It was actually a very interesting display of how ocean currents move. Those ducks had no say in where they were going, though. They were carried by the movement of the water they were in, instead of going to the place where their ship was supposed to take them. Rubber ducks were spotted in England, Spain, South America, Indonesia, and Alaska, and as late as in 2007! Duckies were adrift at sea for 15 years! When we stray from the vehicle that takes us to our destination, we are left to the currents and eddies that twirl around. God's plan for the best way to live is the best plan to follow. When we abandon that plan, the currents of the moment, the circumstances of life, will carry us aimlessly around. Paul's letter to the Ephesians says that is a childish way to live. The mature thing to do is find out what Jesus wants from you and to steer your life in that direction. Then you'll get to your intended destination.

Garbage Tornado

But whatever were gains to me I now consider loss for the sake of Christ. What is more, I consider everything a loss because of the surpassing worth of knowing Christ Jesus my Lord, for whose sake I have lost all things. I consider them garbage, that I may gain Christ and be found in him, not having a righteousness that comes from the law, but that which is through faith in Christ - the righteousness that comes from God on the basis of faith. **Philippians 3:7-9**

On a mission trip to Tijuana, Mexico, some students and I visited a garbage dump, where some very poor people actually lived. When the garbage truck arrived and dumped a new load of trash, many people crowded around to pick through it and look for anything valuable they could sell, or even use in making their homes. While we were there, a wind came through this pit of garbage and swirled around, picking up lightweight papers and wrappers. The result was a whirlwind of trash - it looked like a tornado, but was completely made of trash from the dump. The scene reminded me of this Bible verse, which tells us that all kinds of things we value and cling to as important, compared to knowing Jesus, are garbage. Paul listed his important family, his education, and the way he obeyed the law and acted on his beliefs. All of those things, at one time, made him feel proud, but they are worldly things that don't last. And we look as sad as those poor people clamoring for junk when we run after those things. Instead of focusing on things we can achieve or accumulate in this life, our focus and goal in life should be to know Jesus and have others know him.

Let us throw off everything that hinders and the sin that so easily entangles. And let us run with perseverance the race marked out for us, fixing our eyes on Jesus, the pioneer and perfecter of faith. **Hebrews 12:1-2**

So we fix our eyes not on what is seen, but on what is unseen, since what is seen is temporary, but what is unseen is eternal. **2Corinthians 4:18**

So do not worry, saying, "What shall we eat?" or "What shall we drink?" or "What shall we wear?" For the pagans run after all these things, and your heavenly Father knows that you need them. But seek first His kingdom and His righteousness, and all these things will be given to you as well. **Matthew 6:31-33**

Trial By Fire

Put to death, therefore, whatever belongs to your earthly nature: sexual immorality, impurity, lust, evil desires and greed, which is idolatry. Because of these, the wrath of God is coming. You used to walk in these ways, in the life you once lived. But now you must also rid yourselves of all such things as these: anger, rage, malice, slander, and filthy language from your lips. **Colossians 3:5-17**

Forest fires actually have some benefits: leaves and little dead branches on the ground are burned up, avoiding giant fires in the future and letting light reach shorter plants. Some harmful insects and tree diseases are killed off by fires. Some seeds are dispersed only by fires. Less water is absorbed by plants, so there is more in the streams. The forest is refined and purified, in a way, by fire. In the Bible, refining is often compared to the refining of silver, burning off impurities by heating silver to a very high temperature. How does the refining of our character and our faith happen? Sometimes those really hard circumstances or the consequences of our sin can act like a cleansing fire that destroys ugly things that shouldn't be in our hearts. Our good God asks us to confess and pray to Him and He promises forgiveness and cleansing. Look at the list in Colossians chapter 3 of the things we should put off (put to death, even) and the traits to put on, as believers. We can be healthier after the process has been done.

The words of the Lord are flawless, like silver purified in a crucible, like gold refined seven times. **Psalm 12:6**

See, I have refined you, though not as silver; I have tested you in the furnace of affliction. **Isaiah 48:10**

Some of the wise will stumble, so that they may be refined, purified, and made spotless until the time of the end. **Daniel 11:35**

The Scientific Method

Do not treat prophecies with contempt but test them all; hold on to what is good, reject every kind of evil. **1 Thessalonians 5:20-22**

The Scientific Method is a way that scientists use to test one thing at a time and to base the test on things we already know. I was recently studying worms with 2nd graders. We wanted to find out whether worms prefer light or darkness, and whether they like dry or wet conditions. When we tested for the light question, we had to provide both options for the worms (light and dark) and make sure that everything else (how wet it was) was the same in both places, so that when the worm went left, we knew he was choosing dark, because both the light and dark areas were equally wet or dry. There are a lot of instructions about life in our Bibles. And if we follow Jesus, we have the Holy Spirit to guide us. But there are many times in life when you have to make a decision, or a problem comes up, and there's not a verse directly about that in the Bible. So you get to use the brain God gave you and be a scientist to make your choice. Fortunately for us, God has given us a "control," something that we know to be true, and against which we can measure any other option or decision. It's our Bible. Read these verses about using God's Word as a way to test decisions.

Now the Berean Jews were of more noble character than those in Thessalonica, for they received the message with great eagerness and examined the Scriptures every day to see if what Paul said was true. **Acts 17:11**

All Scripture is God-breathed and is useful for teaching, rebuking, correcting and training in righteousness, so that the servant of God may be thoroughly equipped for every good work. **2Timothy 3:16-17**

The Power of Doubling

Pray for us that the message of the Lord may spread rapidly and be honored, just as it was with you. **2 Thessalonians 3:1**

There is an old story about a man from India who taught the king to play chess. The king was so grateful that he asked the man to name his price for such a wonderful gift. The man asked the king for a "simple" gift of rice. He asked the king to put one grain of rice on a square of the chess board, then 2 grains on the next square, then 4 grains on the next, and so on until all of the squares on the chess board were filled. The king laughed and agreed, not knowing the power of doubling. Had he done some calculations, the king would have seen that at the end of the first row on the board, he'd have given 128 grains of rice. At the end of the second row, he's have given 32,000 grains of rice. At the end of the last row on the checkerboard, he'd have 18 pentillion grains of rice! (18,446,744,073,709,551,615, to be exact - that would fill 174 million Olympic size swimming pools!) Exponential growth is powerful! Jesus described the Kingdom of Heaven growing that way with the mustard seed parable (**Matthew 13:31-32**). That dramatic growth can happen just by doubling, over and over again. Our part in growing God's kingdom is to share Jesus' offer of salvation with other people. If only 1 person accepts it, then our place in the Kingdom has doubled. If you feel alone as a believer, know that God is building a HUGE kingdom! How great that He allows us to help, He certainly doesn't need us.

Everyone who calls on the name of the Lord will be saved. How, then, can they call on the one they have not believed in? And how can they believe in the one of whom they have not heard? And how can they hear without someone preaching to them? And how can anyone preach unless they are sent? As it is written, "How beautiful are the feet of those who bring good news!" **Romans 10:13-15**

Only One Answer

For there is one God and one mediator between God and mankind, the man Christ Jesus. **1Timothy 2:5**

In algebra, there are equations that have just one solution, some that have an infinite number of solutions, and some that have no solution. Some people think that when it comes to God, there is no solution: "God doesn't have any say in my life, He is not the answer", or that any solution is fine: "whatever you believe is good for you." When, in fact, there is only one true God, only one answer to the big questions in life. The Bible states that over and over again.

Salvation is found in no one else, for there is no other name under heaven given to mankind by which we must be saved. **Acts 4:12**

Jesus answered, "I am the way and the truth and the life. No one comes to the Father except through me. **John 14:6**

$3 + x = 5$ x can only equal 2; that's the only number that makes this statement true

$3 + x = 3 + x$ x can be any number because this is true for whatever you substitute for x

$3 + x = 4 + x$ there is no solution for x, no number you could put in there that would make these two sides equal

In Tune With the Spirit

What you heard from me, keep as the pattern of sound teaching, with faith and love in Christ Jesus. Guard the good deposit that was entrusted to you - guard it with the help of the Holy Spirit who lives in us. **2Timothy 1:13-14**

One of my favorite things to do is make music with other people. I played in a classic rock band with my dad when I was in junior high. I sing with a gospel choir, and I play guitar to lead others in singing. The most important thing, when making music with others, is that you keep the same beat and that your instruments are "in tune." So when I play a G chord and the piano player plays a G chord, the sounds agree. There are three ways to tune a musical instrument: you can adjust the different notes on the instrument so that they are in the right relationship to each other, you can match the notes on your instrument to another instrument, or you can adjust your notes to match a tuner, which measures the frequency of the notes to see if they are the true note (for example, the sound wave from an A note should vibrate 440 times per second, whether it's being sung, plucked, or strummed). The Holy Spirit is what tells us the "true note" of how to live. Living "in tune with" the Spirit means matching up with how He guides. If you follow the other methods of tuning, you run the risk of only being ok with yourself (and then when you try to get along with others, it sounds awful!), or you align with another person, who may be flawed in their idea of what's right. Living rightly requires that we make decisions based on the One who says what's right. If we each tune to His perfect pitch, then the dissonant sounds of selfishness and apathy don't wreck the song God has intended.

Since we live by the Spirit, let us keep in step with the Spirit. **Galatians 5:25**

Those who live according to the flesh have their minds set on what the flesh desires; but those who live in accordance with the Spirit have their minds set on what the Spirit desires. **Romans 8:5**

How can a young person stay on the path of purity? By living according to Your word... I have hidden Your word in my heart that I might not sin against You. **Psalm 119:9,11**

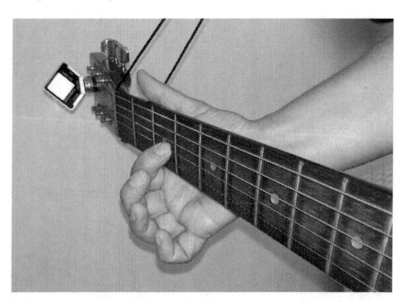

Harmony

Read the whole letter of **Philemon** - it will take less than 10 minutes.

A chord, in music, is two or more notes, played at the same time, which complement each other, and sound good together. This is called harmony. You'll notice if you play an instrument, that some combinations of notes sound pleasant (harmonious) and some sound dissonant, almost painful to the ear. Sound waves come in different sizes, the shorter ones have higher pitches and the longer ones have lower pitches. Interestingly, the notes which sound good together have lengths that are mathematically related. For instance, one note will measure exactly twice as long as another, and those notes blend well to the ear. For people, living in harmony is pleasant, rather than discordant. How can we "tune" or adjust our actions so that we complement the actions of others? We don't need to be exactly the same as someone else to get along with them but live in a way that our lives and our actions combine in pleasing ways.

Live in harmony with one another. Do not be proud, but be willing to associate with people of low position. Do not be conceited. **Romans 12:16**

How good and pleasant it is when God's people live together in unity! **Psalm 133:1**

Let us therefore make every effort to do what leads to peace and mutual edification. **Romans 14:19**

May the God who gives endurance and encouragement give you the same attitude of mind toward each other that Christ Jesus had, so that with one mind and one voice you may glorify the God and Father of our Lord Jesus Christ. **Romans 15:5**

The Master Builder

Jesus had been found worthy of greater honor than Moses, just as the builder of a house has greater honor than the house itself. For every house is built by someone, but God is the builder of everything. **Hebrews 3:3-4**

Building blocks like Legos or Zoob can make lots of different things, in their different combinations. Natural elements (the 100 or so of them on the periodic table) are the same way, in that they make up everything. Everything is built from them and then breaks down into them. This is the Cosmic Recycling System that God has created! The elements in a banana peel get broken down in the worm bin and turned into soil, which then nourishes a growing blueberry bush and then gets mixed into muffins, and then consumed by you, … If you think about it, that's how God could finish creating on the sixth day and still have things running all these millennia later! This is super amazing, but the elements are not worth our worship. Only God, the "Builder of the house," the Creator of the elements, the Designer of the Universe!

Eyes

Therefore, since we are surrounded by such a great cloud of witnesses, let us throw off everything that hinders and the sin that so easily entangles. And let us run with perseverance the race marked out for us, fixing our eyes on Jesus, the pioneer and perfecter of our faith.
Hebrews 12:1-2

Your eyeball is essentially a dark room with one small window. The black circle in the middle of your eye is that window - it's not actually black, but transparent, but there's no light coming from inside your eye, so it looks black. In fact, you can simulate traveling into your eyeball by turning off all the lights in a room and covering all of the windows except for a small opening, maybe the size of a playing card. On the wall opposite that small opening, you should see images from the other side of the window: trees rustling in the breeze, cars driving by. Send your friend out there to wave to you! … and they'll all be upside down. Just like in this eye model, the images that enter our eye, focus upside-down on our retinas, a light-sensitive screen on the back of our eyeballs. Sensors in the retina send messages to the brain, where the images are interpreted as things you recognize. Jesus calls the eyes the lamp of the body. He wasn't talking about the light rays entering your pupil or about how your eyes physically work, but about what you pay attention to, day to day. We usually look at things we pay attention to - didn't your mom ever say to you, "Look at me when I'm talking to you!" - she wanted to know you were paying attention. These four passages describe that same idea. Look them up. What is it that they say we should be looking at, and therefore paying attention to? [**2Corinthians 4:18; Ephesians 1:18; Philippians 3:17; Hebrews 12:2**]

Direct me in the path of Your commands, for there I find delight. Turn my heart toward Your statutes and not toward selfish gain. Turn my eyes away from worthless things; preserve my life according to Your word. **Psalm 119:35-37**

I made a covenant with my eyes not to look lustfully at a young woman. **Job 31:1**

Evaluating Sources

If any of you lacks wisdom, you should ask God, who gives generously to all without finding fault, and it will be given to you. **James 1:5**

Did your teacher ever assign a research project and tell you to use a certain number of sources, but then require that you make sure the sources are reliable? It's increasingly important with the invention of the internet, where just anyone can post just anything, in a matter of minutes and at no cost! When you're quoting the knowledge of others, it's important to make sure they know what they're talking about. This is using wisdom, the ability to discern right from wrong and good from bad. God is the source of wisdom, "the fear of the Lord is the beginning of wisdom," says the Proverb. The book of Job contains a conversation between Job and his friends, who are not correct in the things they're saying about Job's situation (nor about some of the things they say about God). Job's friend Eliphaz was using his own observations and conclusions. Job's friend Bildad quoted the wisdom of past generations. And Job's friend Zophar's strategy was to seek out wise people.* Check your source. A Google search won't help you find wisdom; ask God.

My son, if you accept my words and store up my commands within you, turning your ear to wisdom and applying your heart to understanding - indeed, if you call out for insight and cry aloud for understanding, and if you look for it as for silver and search for it as for hidden treasure, then you will understand the fear of the Lord and find the knowledge of God. For the Lord gives wisdom; from His mouth come knowledge and understanding. **Proverbs 2:1-6**

The Spirit of the Lord will rest on him - the Spirit of wisdom and of understanding, the Spirit of counsel and of might, the Spirit of the knowledge and fear of the Lord - and he will delight in the fear of the Lord. **Isaiah 11:2-3**

Do not be wise in your own eyes; fear the Lord and shun evil. **Proverbs 3:7**

(read also **Job 28:12-28; 1Cor 1:18-25**)

*this idea is from the NIV Life Application Bible, Tyndale

Mmm, Mmm, Good

Like newborn babies, crave pure spiritual milk, so that by it you may grow up in your salvation, now that you have tasted that the Lord is good. **1Peter 2:2-3**

Taste happens when chemicals go onto your tongue and sensors there send signals to your brain, to catalog and remember for later. Think of the taste of french fries, or chocolate, or watermelon Jolly Rancher. Our sense of taste is tied to memory. Have you ever tasted something and it brought back a memory of your childhood or a certain person? There is a smoothie place near me that sells a "50/50" shake, which is orange and vanilla. It reminds me of the children's aspirin I took when I was 5 or 6 years old! It's amazing how clear the memory is! 3 out of 7 passages that showed up in a word search on "good" in the Bible, showed "taste" in the passage, as well. Isn't that an interesting connection? Experiencing the goodness of the Lord and of His Word makes you crave it and remember it and recognize it when you encounter it later. What a wonderful taste to remember!

Taste and see that the Lord is good; blessed is the one who takes refuge in Him. **Psalm 34:8**

It is impossible for those who have once been enlightened, who have tasted the heavenly gift, who have shared in the Holy Spirit, who have tasted the goodness of the word of God and the powers of the coming age and who have fallen away, to be brought back to repentance. **Hebrews 6:5**

You are good and what You do is good; teach me Your decrees. **Psalm 119:68**

How God Made You

Each of you should use whatever gift you have received to serve others, as faithful stewards of God's grace in its various forms. If anyone speaks, they should do so as one who speaks the very words of God. If anyone serves, they should do so with the strength God provides, so that in all things God may be praised through Jesus Christ. **1Peter 4:10-11**

I have three children, and while it's obvious that they are siblings, their personalities, interests, and strengths are very different from one another. One of my children is very visually perceptive. He notices everything! Another is musically inclined, talks to himself when he's nervous and can imitate sounds really well. Our third is a tactile learner who has always liked taking things apart. She often does her homework, sitting on top of a chair back or on the floor. God made each of my 3 kids differently, and just as with you and me, He did it on purpose. Knowing your strengths and tendencies can help you interact with people, find projects or jobs you enjoy, and also inform how you worship God. Some people LOVE to sing songs of praise to God, but others just aren't that into music or get too worried about their bad singing voice to enjoy that. While it's nice to try different modes of praising God, sometimes the most sincere and genuine praise will come when we do what we're good at and enjoy. Worship Him *for* the way He made you, get to know Him *in* the way He made you, and serve Him *by* the way He made you.

For You created my inmost being; You knit me together in my mother's womb. I praise You because I am fearfully and wonderfully made; Your works are wonderful, I know that full well... Your eyes saw my unformed body; all the days ordained for me were written in Your book before one of them came to be. **Psalm 139:13-14,16**

We have different gifts, according to the grace given to each of us. If your gift is prophesying, then prophesy in accordance with your faith. If it is serving, then serve; if it is teaching, then teach; if it is to encourage, then give encouragement; if it is giving, then give generously; if it is to lead, do it diligently, if it is to show mercy, do it cheerfully. **Romans 12:4-8**

Cornerstone

As you come to him, the living Stone - rejected by humans but chosen by God and precious to Him - you also, like living stones, are being built into a spiritual house to be a holy priesthood, offering spiritual sacrifices acceptable to God through Jesus Christ. For in Scripture it says: "See, I lay a stone in Zion, a chosen and precious cornerstone, and the one who trusts in him will never be put to shame." **1Peter 2:4-6**

When building a stone or brick building, there is an important part of the first layer, called the cornerstone. It needs to be very square and true and placed exactly where the builder wants the corner to be. All other bricks, and eventually walls, are lined up according to this stone's sides. Likewise, in an arch, there is a stone called the capstone or the keystone, which is the LAST brick placed and holds all the others together with the force of gravity that acts on it. Both of these stones are significant. Jesus is compared to both of these, he is said to be a stone the builders rejected - Jewish leaders denied him when he was on earth - and it turns out he's the most important. When the church of Jesus is compared to a building, in 1Peter, Jesus is the cornerstone, the One with whom we must all align ourselves, so that the building is true and solid.

Consequently, you are no longer foreigners and strangers, but fellow citizens with God's people and also member of His household, built on the foundation of the apostles and prophets, with Christ Jesus himself as the chief cornerstone. In him the whole building is joined together and rises to become a holy temple in the Lord. And in him you too are being built together to become a dwelling in which God lives by His Spirit. **Ephesians 2:19-22**

Jesus is " the stone you builders rejected, which has become the cornerstone." **Acts 4:11**

Fiction vs. Nonfiction Books

For prophecy never had its origin in the human will, but prophets, though human, spoke from God as they were carried along by the Holy Spirit. **2Peter 1:21**

Most of the Bible is non-fiction, a historical account of real people who lived in real places and really followed God (or failed to) in their lives on earth. Just like nonfiction books are researched and evidence is collected before they are published, the Bible has lots of evidence and research to support its truth. Archaeologists have found evidence of groups of people that are written about in the Bible: names, places, routes traveled, and customs of the day, that match up with Biblical history. The description of the blind man's healing that's described in Mark 8, matches with medical documentation today of "post-blind syndrome," where newly-sighted people see blurry images at first before their vision clears up. There are more copies of the New Testament than other ancient documents that historians accept as reliable. Just because no one mentioned in the Bible is still around to talk to, doesn't mean that they didn't really live and do just what it says they did in the pages of Scripture. So let's not talk of Bible "characters" or "stories," because that makes it sound like it's fiction. Yes, there are some parts of Scripture that are meant to be stories or poems or songs or visions, but those parts are clearly described as such. The Bible is full of geographical information, history, real-people biographies, accounts of real political leaders, descriptions of how things work, poetry, philosophy, and diaries. Yes, there is a talking donkey and visions of other places no human has visited, but they are real and really happened. The gospel is not made up.

I want you to know, brothers and sisters, that the gospel I preached is not of human origin. I did not receive it from any man, nor was

I taught it; rather, I received it by revelation from Jesus Christ. **Galatians 1:11-12**

"You are out of your mind, Paul!" [Governor Festus] shouted. "Your great learning is driving you insane." "I am not insane, most excellent Festus," Paul replied, "What I am saying is true and reasonable." **Acts 26:24-25**

Planting a Seed So That It Dies

This is how we know what love is: Jesus Christ laid down his life for us. And we ought to lay down our lives for our brothers and sisters. **1John 3:16**

Have you ever thought about this when you've planted seeds in soil? In order to produce more of the plant, a part of another plant has to die and be buried. I put seeds in the ground to grow some flowers and there was nothing to see, no growth or change, for weeks! Then, a small sprout popped up out of the ground, then a small stem, then some leaves, and the plant grew and grew. It looked nothing like the small, hard, round seed I put in the ground. Jesus used this picture to show what he was doing by dying on the cross. The ultimate evidence of love, stated many times in the Bible, is self-sacrifice.

Very truly I tell you, unless a kernel of wheat falls to the ground and dies, it remains only a single seed. But if it dies, it produces many seeds. **John 12:24**

This is love: not that we loved God, but that He loved us and sent His Son as an atoning sacrifice for our sins. **1John 4:10**

Greater love has no one than this: to lay down one's life for one's friends. **John 15:13**

Because of His great love for us, God, who is rich in mercy, made us alive with Christ even when we were dead in transgressions. **Ephesians 2:4**

A Cellular Doxology

To the only God our Savior be glory, majesty, power and authority, through Jesus Christ our Lord, before all ages, now and forevermore! Amen. **Jude 1:25**

Cells are like the building blocks of living things. Although their sizes vary throughout the human body, a cell's size can be approximated like this: If you look at the thickness of your fingernail, that's about 1mm. The size of an average cell in your body is about $1/100^{th}$ of that! The study of human cells is an amazing voyage into a tiny city with all kinds of workers and buildings and transportation vehicles. Cells have jobs and God designed them to work in a certain way. The parts inside a cell also have jobs and those parts all work together to make the cell function as it should. Find the video called "The Inner Life of the Cell," made by Harvard University, and watch the animation created to show all that's going on in the cell. (You can find a narrated version, which has all of the science-y words that describe what's going on, or you can watch the un-narrated version and just enjoy the show.) Did you know all of that was going on inside your body, times 37 trillion? All the time? God designed all the parts of a cell to perform different jobs and work together, just like he gave people different gifts, to contribute to society and to the church. What has God designed you to do? Or what role or gift has come to you, since becoming a Christian? He means for you to use it in the Body of Christ, to glorify Him, and to complement all of the other people in it.

For You knit me together in my mother's womb. I praise You because I am fearful and wonderfully made; Your works are wonderful, I know that full well. **Psalm 139:13-14**

Oh, the depths of the riches of the wisdom and knowledge of God! How unsearchable His judgements, and His paths are beyond tracing out! "Who has known the mind of the Lord? Or who has been His counselor?" "Who has ever given to God, that God should repay them?" For from Him and through Him and for Him are all things. To Him be glory forever! Amen. **Romans 11:33-36**

Alpha and Omega

"I am the Alpha and the Omega," says the Lord God, "who is, and who was, and who is to come, the Almighty." **Revelation 1:8**

Do you speak another language? Did you know the Bible wasn't written in English? Or that the English language didn't even exist when the Bible was written? Every language that's written down has spelling rules and grammar, and alphabets. In John's revelation of the activities in heaven and glimpses of Jesus on his throne, he hears Jesus say he is the Alpha and Omega. Three times, in Revelation, Jesus says that about himself. What does that mean? Those are the first and last letters of the Greek alphabet. It's like he's saying he is king and source of all, from A to Z. He's eternal and all-inclusive, because he also added, "who was, and is, and is to come." Look at the Greek letters, printed here. If you want to see the Hebrew alphabet, it is found in Psalm 119, as that chapter is written as an acrostic poem, with each stanza starting with one letter of the Hebrew alphabet.

In the beginning was the Word, and the Word was with God, and the Word was God. He was with God in the beginning. Through him all things were made; without him nothing was made that has been made. **John 1:1-3**

This is the one I spoke about when I said, "He who comes after me has surpassed me because he was before me." **John 1:15**

For in him all things were created: things in heaven and on earth, visible and invisible, whether thrones or powers or rulers or authorities; all things have been created through him and for him. He is before all things, and in him all things hold together. **Col 1:16-17**

He said to me, "It is done. I am the Alpha and the Omega, the Beginning and the End." **Revelation 21:6**

"I am the Alpha and the Omega, the First and the Last, the Beginning and the End." **Revelation 22:13**

αβγδεζηθικλμνξοπρστυφχψω
(lower case Greek alphabet)

ΑΒΓΕΖΗΘΙΚΛΜΝΞΟΠΣΦΧΨΩ
(upper case Greek alphabet)

Acknowledgments

Thank you, Mary Osgood, for suggesting MondayChapel. I had no idea, back then, that it would be such a blessing in my life for so many years!

And to the staff and families at Coastline Christian Academy, for all of your encouragement.

Mom, I'm sorry for all the years I asked you NOT to proofread my writing. You're terrific at it! Thanks for your help!

Printed in the United States
by Baker & Taylor Publisher Services